Activity-Based Training Design

To Sharon and Stu

Activity-Based Training Design

Transforming the Learning of Knowledge

JOHN RODWELL

Published by
Gower Publishing Limited
Gower House
Croft Road
Aldershot
Hampshire
GU11 3HR
England

Gower Publishing Company
Suite 420
101 Cherry Street
Burlington
VT 05401-4405
USA

British Library Cataloguing in Publication Data
Rodwell, John
    Activity-based training : transforming the learning
of knowledge
    1. Employees - Training of 2. Active learning
    I. Title
    658.3'124'04

    ISBN-13: 9780566087967

Library of Congress Cataloging-in-Publication Data
Rodwell, John
    Activity-based training : transforming the learning of knowledge / by John Rodwell
        p. cm
    ISBN 978-0-566-08796-7 (alk. paper)
    1. Employees--Training of--Study and teaching--Activity progams. 2. Activity programs in education. 3. Experiential learning. I. Title

    HF5549.5.T7R5627 2007
    658.3'12404

                                                                    2007009759

Printed and bound in Great Britain by TJ International Ltd, Padstow, Cornwall.

Contents

Introduction   1

Part 1: The Design Process

TRAINING ACTIVITIES

Part 2: Active Reading Materials

Part 3: Card-Sort Activities

Part 4: Games and Activity Boards

Conclusion

List of Figures

List of Tables

Acknowledgements

My thanks and love to the following colleagues and friends:

To Anne Hyde for the help and encouragement she gave at the beginning of this writing adventure, and to Julie Smith for the help and encouragement she gave towards the end of this writing adventure.

To Martin, Julie, Helen, Steph and Ian for the inspiration and joy that is 104a.

To Mandie, Anne, Paula, John, Simon, and Anna for making up the original CO L&D Magnificent Seven and helping to make everything in this book become a reality, and to Helen for her unending support.

Introduction

TIMES CHANGE

In the 1990s I wrote a book called *Participative Training Skills*. This book described a range of classroom training methods that could be used instead of the traditional presentation/input/lecture/'chalk and talk'/'pour and snore' still common at the time (and in fact are not uncommon methods I wrote about included buzz groups, syndicates, case fishbowl exercises, and so on.

exercise then, and even now, would be to ask groups of w to a room with flipchart paper and pens with instructions ion that you had posed, and come back with their answers per to review.

This was indeed a great step forward from simply standing up at the front and presenting information to people. The learners were *participating*: they were *thinking things through for themselves*: they were *learning from each other.* This was much better than what had gone before with the straight presentation or lecturing approach.

However, whilst all of these methodologies are still valid and widely used today, I have always had the feeling that there was something missing from them, some essential spark that only seemed to be present with an exceptionally enthusiastic and engaged group. I wondered therefore if there was a way of getting that spark, that level of engagement, more often and from groups that had less natural enthusiasm.

After a while I became conscious that it was not the *processes* of the methodologies that were missing something – it was the *content*. The methods themselves were fine. It was what people were being asked to do that was not. It was the content of the exercises that was often inherently, to be frank – dull.

Something also stuck me about the use of 'participative methods' when used in the way I have described above. It didn't always help people learn the things you wanted them to learn and understand. This feeling related mainly to the way that we dealt with the learning of *knowledge*. The methods used to enable the practising of skills and behaviours (role plays, fishbowls and so on) have always maintained their effectiveness when applied appropriately.

When thinking about the methods used to promote the learning of knowledge, it struck me that we were often simply asking people to play a guessing game. We had the answers written down in our training modules, and we asked questions to bring out these 'learning points'. The trainer's role seemed largely to be about devising the right kind of questions to get the right kind of answers. In practice this was, and remains, a very difficult task indeed. It takes a great deal of skill, time and energy to phrase a question to get a particular kind of answer that you want.

Furthermore, a poorly phrased question could push people down a route that led to inappropriate responses, confusion and frustration for trainers and learners alike. I have seen many trainers end up chest-deep in swamps of this nature and who have had to struggle like mad to extricate themselves. I have been stuck in such swamps on numerous occasions myself!

THE TWO PROBLEMS

So, we have two major problems with the participative training methods that ask groups to consider a question and provide the answer(s).

*   They are not often particularly exciting or engaging.
*   They do not always enable the desired learning outcomes to be achieved.

Here is a true-life example of an approach I took to deal with the two problems.

When running trainer-training events, a key session (ironically) was one on 'Types of Questions', and their use in the training environment. The learning points covered:

- the names of the various types of question and their definitions
- examples of each type of question
- the extent to which they should be used in training.

This session was often delivered as a question-and-answer session, with questions being asked by the trainer, who then usually wrote up the answers on a flipchart. Something like the following might happen:

Trainer: Can anyone tell me what an 'open' question is?

Learner 1: A question that is open-ended and allows people to talk.

Trainer: Thank you, yes. It's a question that often begins with Who What How Why or When. Can anyone give me an example?

Learner 2: How did you decide on your holiday destination this year?

Trainer: Yes, good example. Now do you think this is a type of question we need to use as trainers and why or why not?

Learner 3: Yes, because we can hear what people think and get a feel for how much knowledge and understanding they have.

Trainer: Indeed, so this is a type of question we should use a lot. Now, to move on, can anyone give me a description and an example of a 'closed' question?

Learner 4: A question that asks for a narrower response like: *Should you send off the claim form immediately?*

Trainer: Yes exactly. A question that often asks for a yes/no or a single-word answer. So when should we use these questions, if at all?

Learner 4: Never: people can just guess.

Trainer: Well, there might be occasions when you could use them; can you think when this might be? Anyone?

And so it would go on (and on) through the question types: leading/multiple/ probing/hypothetical/testing/rhetorical etc. Some answers would be appropriate, and some not. It was hard work even when the group came up with good answers. It was even harder work when they came up with wayward answers, or no answers at all.

The session was something of a slog for both the group and the trainer, even though it ticked the box as being participative and *getting the answers from them.*

There had to be a better way.

TRANSFORMATION

The way that this session was transformed into one that was activity based involved looking back at the objective of the session, which was about participants being able to identify the various types of questions to be used in training, and those that should be used with care or avoided completely.

This led to the idea of a small group activity where the groups would be given all the information on cards, and their task would be to sort them into the correct order.

Sets of cards were subsequently produced showing:

*   the name of each type of question
*   a definition of each type
*   an example of each type.

The groups were also given circular 'traffic light' cards that were to be used to indicate if the type of question should be used frequently (green) rarely or with caution (amber) or avoided altogether (red).

Armed with the sets of cards, the groups set about sticking them up on flipcharts to make a chart showing all the question names, definitions, examples and so on.

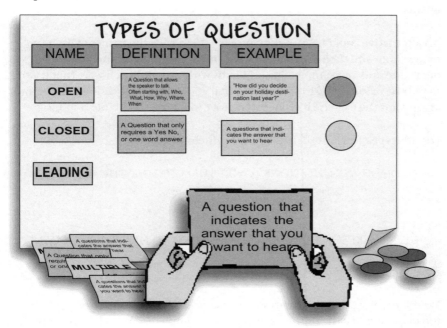

With this change of approach the session had a much greater 'buzz' about it. There was far more discussion and animation in the way the task was carried out. Cards were put into one place, discussed and moved to another place. There was movement, there was noise, there was touching and holding of the card materials, there was colour and there was learning.

People who liked being active (the doers) were able to be active and 'do'. People who liked to be less active (the thinkers) were also able to operate in their preferred style by picking up one or two cards to ponder upon for themselves, and then offer their thoughts on where they should be placed.

The difference in the atmosphere generated by the old question-and-answer approach, and the new card-sort activity-based approach was amazing. And the new approach wasn't rocket science by any stretch of the imagination. It was just a different way of meeting the objectives of the session just using pieces of printed card.

It was from this activity that the concepts of name/definition/example (NDE) cards and traffic lights were developed as activity-based methods in their own right (see Activities 8 and 9 later in this book).

By giving out the cards with all the learning information written on them, the session time was spent examining and discussing *them*, which, in my view, led to a greater understanding of the subject matter than did the question-and-answer approach.

An alternative could have been to provide them with the names of each type of question, and then ask them to write up on the flipchart their ideas of a definition and an example. The problems with this approach were that it would have taken a long time to complete, and it could have been difficult to monitor and review the exercise if groups were not producing acceptable responses.

For this type of exercise, therefore, the principle became:

DON'T ASK QUESTIONS TO GET THEM TO FIND THE ANSWERS

BUT

GIVE THEM THE ANSWERS AND GET THEM TO FIND THEIR *MEANING.*

The benefits

When initially using this method, I had concerns that the activity would be too obvious and easy for the participants to complete. I was relieved to find that this was not the case. In fact I was relieved to notice that most groups would put some cards in the wrong positions. Usually there would be additional thought and debate given to these cards when it was discovered that other cards, not yet placed, would not fit anywhere else. Sometimes a group would need some prompting by the facilitator, but invariably they were able to work out where everything fitted eventually.

When groups completed the card activities, another advantage of using them became apparent: it led to a sense of *achievement*. In front of them was a completed and *visible* piece of work – correctly and accurately constructed after a good deal of thought and debate. It was looked upon with noticeable signs of satisfaction, as if the participants had just put the last piece of a large jigsaw puzzle into place.

You can see from this example how existing training sessions can be transformed into activity-based sessions to accelerate the learning of knowledge. Whilst the materials may take time to produce beforehand, the use of the activities can save a great deal of classroom time.

In these times when there is huge pressure on managers and employees to deliver results and meet targets, training can be sidelined if it is felt that the end results cannot justify the time and expense of releasing people to attend.

There is a good chance that activity-based training will:

- reduce classroom time (from three days to two for example);
- increase the amount of knowledge learned;
- be more memorable as a positive learning experience;
- be more enjoyable for the participants;
- be more enjoyable for the trainer.

What more could you ask for?

Part 1
The Design Process

CHAPTER 1

Learning Styles and Fun

O ne of the main reasons why activity-based methods work is that they are fun! Another is that they appeal to a range of different senses, and subsequently appeal to individuals' different learning styles.

THE FUN FACTOR

Training is a serious business. A lot of money is either spent or invested (depending on your point of view) in it and it has to produce results and measurable benefits for the organization otherwise you might as well not bother at all and spend (or invest) your money on something else.

However, although it is agreed that training is a serious business, it does not mean that you have to be dour and miserable as you do it. It doesn't mean that you can't have any fun or enjoyment while you are learning. Indeed I am sure that most scholars and adult learning experts would agree that a relaxed and open environment is almost a prerequisite of effective learning.

The activity-based training methods described in this book have been designed to be enjoyed not just by the participants but also by the learning facilitator or trainer.

The serious side to the issue is that the training must also do its job. It must facilitate the learning of the knowledge and skills needed by the people who are on the receiving end, which must in turn lead on towards the appropriate application in the workplace, and the required organizational outcomes.

I have known people come back from training events who have said something like 'It was great fun and I learned a lot'. This is how it should be. I have also known people on the other hand who have returned from training events saying: 'It was so boring! I didn't learn a thing!' This is obviously unacceptable. Also unacceptable, however, is the type of training where someone comes back and says: 'Didn't learn anything really, but it was great fun!'

The term 'serious fun' has been coined for the development of computer-based training that works like a computer game and captures the interest and imagination of people in just the way that computer games do. I believe that the same term can be applied to classroom and any other kind of training.

LEARNING STYLES

The methods described in this book also promote learning in the way that they can appeal to different senses, and thus different learning styles.

Within the neuro linguistic programming (NLP) school of psychology, the concept of individuals having certain 'modalities' is put forward. A modality can be described as being the way that you perceive and take on board information most easily. According to NLP principles, there are three main learning modalities. These are visual, auditory and kinaesthetic.

Visual

If you have a preference for visual learning, you will prefer to learn through seeing and using your eyes. Here are a few other attributes of visual learners:

- They will remember what they see rather than what they hear or touch or feel.
- They prefer written instructions to verbal (and may therefore write verbal instructions down).
- They will memorize things by making visual associations.
- They are not easily distracted by noise.

Auditory

If you have a preference for auditory learning, you will prefer to learn through hearing and using your ears. Here are a few attributes of auditory learners:

- They will remember what was discussed more than what was seen or touched or felt.
- They can remember and follow verbal instructions easily.
- They are better at talking than writing.
- They can remember not only things that were said, but also their tone and pitch.
- They are easily distracted by noise.

Kinaesthetic

If you have a preference for kinaesthetic learning, you will prefer to learn through moving, doing and touching. Here are a few attributes of kinaesthetic learners:

- They will remember the manipulation and movement of objects.
- They can memorize by pacing around and seeing.
- They like games they can get involved in.
- They respond to physical rewards and prizes.
- They like to act things out.

According to strict NLP psychology, there are two other modalities: olfactory (smell) and gustatory (taste). Whilst not impossible to promote learning through these two senses in a classroom environment, it is not so easy, and there are not very many people who naturally learn best through either of these senses.

When you start to look at the activity-based methods in this book, you will see that many of the activities appeal to at least two of these modalities, if not all three at the same time. Here is one example from each type of activity described in this book:

Missing bullet points (active reading)

- Reading/checking for the right place – visual.
- Discussing with others – auditory.
- Cutting and/or pasting – kinaesthetic.

Washing line (card sort)

- Seeing different colours, shapes and graphic text – visual.
- Discussing with others/listening to instructions – auditory.
- Handling the different shaped items and pegging onto the line – kinaesthetic.

What am I? (games and activity boards)

- Seeing coloured cards and graphic text, watching demonstrations – visual.
- Listening to verbal clues and descriptions, listening to demonstrations – auditory.
- Handling of cards, moving and acting out the demonstrations – kinaesthetic.

ACCELERATED LEARNING

The methods described in this book also comply with many of the principles of Accelerated Learning, a movement which fortunately seems to be getting more and more of a foothold into organizational learning and training.

Here are some of the Accelerated Learning principles with which I believe the activity-based methods in this book comply:

Use of all the senses

As described above with the NLP learning modalities.

Positive learning environment

The methods promote a relaxed yet engaging learning environment along with moments of childlike excitement and feelings of achievement when activities are completed.

Collaboration

All of the activities can be carried out by small groups working in collaboration.

Variety

The activity-based methods are of sufficient number to allow for a variety of activities just using them alone. Further variety can be added, however, through the use of more traditional participative and presentational methods.

Working with the brain

The human brain thrives on being stimulated through things like colour, movement, texture, shape, rhythm, sounds and so on. The brain also works better with imagery rather than words. People will remember more about the activities and their content because there is more to trigger their recall.

***

As yet I have no scientific proof that Accelerated Learning or activity-based training enables people to learn more than any other methods. However, even if there was absolutely no difference between the amount of learning achieved through the new methods and the old methods, and the only difference was the amount of enjoyment and fun experienced by the participants, I know which methods I would prefer, both as participant and trainer!

LEARNING STYLES
AND FUN

Outcome-Based Training Design

THE TRAINING CYCLE

The concept of the training cycle model shown in Figure 2.1 will not be new to most trainers. It is the basic model for the provision of training. In essence, the training cycle plots the development processes required to produce effective training and is often seen as progressing in four distinct stages.

1   You identify the needs.
2   You design the training to meet the needs.
3   You deliver what you have designed.
4   You evaluate the results.

Figure 2.1   The training cycle

It is not within the scope of this book to delve very deeply into the processes and considerations relating to all four stages, but I will discuss some of the key issues surrounding each stage and lead towards showing where activity-based training design fits within the cycle in general, and the design stage in particular.

NEEDS ANALYSIS AND EVALUATION CRITERIA

Sometimes the four-stage approach of the training cycle can mislead trainers into thinking that the evaluation stage is *only* to be considered after the training needs have been identified and the training has been designed and delivered. It isn't.

It is vital to establish the evaluation criteria (or the *required outcomes*) for any training during the early *needs analysis* stage. The evaluation criteria should be identified at both organizational and individual levels.

Organizational outcomes

Ideally, all training and learning activities should be directly linked to the achievement of specific organizational objectives. Sometimes this can be reasonably straightforward, sometimes not.

Organizational evaluation criteria can be established most easily where *quantitative* measures can be applied. Thus some organizational evaluation criteria could be:

- 'To decrease production time of Product X by 10 per cent.'
- 'To decrease average sickness absence days per year from eight days per person to five days per person.'

Once such criteria have been established (and it has been agreed that training is the most appropriate solution) the results of the training can be evaluated against the criteria at a reasonable time after it has been delivered. A reasonable time could be anything from around three months to a year or more depending on the nature of the training and the criteria.

More difficult to establish are the organizational evaluation criteria or outcomes for training that may not have a direct link to operational objectives.

Sometimes, organizations have a perceived need to improve the capability of their managers in certain areas but find it difficult to be more specific about the desired organizational benefits that should be achieved by doing so, and how they will be measured. In such situations it may be better to consider the evaluation criteria at an *individual* level only and accept that benefits to the organization will follow, even if they can only be vaguely described and not specifically measurable.

Individual outcomes

Evaluation criteria at an individual level are best written as statements of what the individual participants will be able to *do* as a result of the training. These statements then become some of the overall objectives of the training. These objectives can then be evaluated perhaps some three to six months after the training has been received.

Some examples of what participants will be able to do by the end of the training (not necessarily related to each other) could be:

- Give and receive feedback on performance and personal feedback in accordance with given guidelines.
- Apply relevant assertiveness techniques when dealing with difficult situations involving colleagues, staff or customers and avoid inappropriate aggressiveness and passivity.
- Apply the contents of the organization's new code of conduct by producing an effective risk assessment; identifying breaches by staff, colleagues and managers and acting accordingly when breaches occur.

Note that the main thrust of these objective statements is to describe the *actions* or *skills* that the participants will need to perform. The training may also need to cover any underpinning *knowledge* or other skills to enable these actions to be conducted effectively.

Even if you have a good set of organizational evaluation criteria, the required outcomes of the training at an individual level will still need to be set. In this case, the individual outcomes will need to work towards meeting the organizational outcomes.

CUTTING THE TRAINING CYCLE

If we now take another look at the training cycle, we can see that it is possible to cut it into a simplified two-stage model to encapsulate the 'before and after' approach to setting evaluation criteria early in the process and then identifying the extent to which they have been met after the training has been designed and delivered.

Figure 2.2   The cut-down training cycle

This approach has been called an 'outcomes-based approach' as it concentrates on what the outcomes of the training must be. Too often, training is designed on an 'input-based approach' whereby the training topics or the content of the training are included in the programme because they look like they might be relevant. The kinds of thought processes that can result in the input-based approach go something like this:

Designer 1: We've been asked from 'on high' to design a three-day course for managers on time management. What can we put in it?

Designer 2: Well, there's that material we've got on how to make the most of your diary, we could use that – and we've got that really funny video about delegation.

Designer 1: Great! Anything else we can throw in?

Designer 2: What about speed reading? We've got something on that.

Designer 1: Yes, that would be good, and of course there's that model with that Important/Not important/Urgent/Not urgent grid. That's gone down really well before.

Designer 2: Great idea! People liked that mind mapping stuff as well; I think we should include that too. We can also put in those sessions on handling your paperwork, and how to manage your electronic files and folders. That should fill up the three days easily.

Designer 1: Sounds good to me. I think we've got our programme!

The problem with this kind of scenario of course is that requests for training can come down from 'on high' in just this way! If someone had been able to ask questions about what the managers needed to be able to *do* as a result of the training, just possibly, something along the lines of the following objective statements might have emerged:

As a result of the training, managers will be able to:

- *apply relevant planning and prioritizing tools to manage their daily, weekly and monthly workloads to meet their targets;*
- *use appropriate techniques for minimizing interruptions and distractions;*
- *negotiate with higher managers to avoid excessive workloads and unrealistic deadlines.*

The previous scattergun approach would no doubt have met with some success. Some of the topics would have been relevant to some people at some point in time. However, with the 'required outcomes' in mind, the training design process can be much more focused and concentrate on achieving the required outcomes *only*, without any unnecessary padding. (And it might only need two days!)

Whether at organizational or individual level, the evaluation criteria (the required outcomes) need to be established *before* any training is designed. Some form of needs analysis, whether formal or informal, or even using the knowledge and experience of you and others, must be carried out in order to ensure that:

- the training can be specifically designed to work towards the achieving the evaluation criteria or required outcomes;
- the people who receive the training can be made aware of its purpose before they attend;
- any future evaluation project will be able to focus on identifying the extent to which the evaluation criteria have been met. (Which could simplify the process considerably.)

KNOWLEDGE AND SKILLS

Once you have established what people need to be able to *do* as a result of their training, you can then establish what they need to *know* to help them to do it, and also if there are any additional underpinning or generic skills that are needed.

It is possible on occasion to forget that the actions people take in order to do their jobs are actually skills. (Good face-to-face communication skills will be needed by managers to handle appraisal interviews effectively, but they will also need the skill to fill in the documentation correctly and on time.)

When identifying the *knowledge* needed, you should always keep the objective statements in mind. Just about *everything* contained in any training programme should be able to be traced back to one or more of the objective statements.

TYPES OF KNOWLEDGE

There can be different kinds of knowledge that people may need to learn. Here are some ideas of what the different kinds could be:

Theoretical knowledge

This is the kind of knowledge you can get from books and attending lectures and seminars and so on. People will be learning about theories and models on topics like:

- leadership

- motivation
- communication
- learning styles
- managing change.

On its own, this kind of knowledge can be of limited use. It is the kind of knowledge that has eventually to be considered and *used* in order to be of benefit to the individual and the organization.

Technical/procedural knowledge

Technical and procedural knowledge becomes a *skill* when it is put to practical use in a real situation. Someone could have all the knowledge about how something *should* be done – but may not have developed the skill of *applying* it in practice. In the work environment, such knowledge (and skills) could include:

- using IT/software applications
- project management
- performance management
- interviewing
- report writing
- researching
- coaching and training others.

In order for the technique or procedure to be carried out effectively as a skill, the necessary knowledge has to be learned in the first place.

Background knowledge

This can include knowledge about your organization and work issues, such as:

- role/objectives
- structure

- the work of other divisions
- the work of other teams
- the culture of the organization
- clients or customers
- background information on projects
- policies
- the law.

TYPES OF SKILL

As with knowledge, there can be different kinds of skill that people may need to learn. Here are some ideas on how the different kinds of skill could be described:

Physical/manual skills

These will include a wide range of skills in areas such as:

- manufacturing
- engineering
- factory/other processing
- maintenance
- building and construction
- machine operation.

This type of skill may be less common in an office environment, although there are some forms of physical skills that could be required such as:

- manual handling of loads
- keyboard/typing skills
- maintenance and repair
- use of machinery and equipment.

Personal skills

These are the 'thinking' or 'mental' types of skill that we often need to apply at the workplace. They include skills like:

- planning
- time management
- decision-making
- problem-solving
- creative thinking
- coping with change.

In all of these areas there are specific tools and techniques that can be learned and applied at work.

Interpersonal skills

These are the 'face-to-face' skills that we need to employ when dealing with other people in situations such as:

- team and other meetings
- performance reviews
- conducting negotiations
- dealing with customers
- training
- interviewing
- general day-to-day contact.

The kinds of skill that come under this heading include:

- building rapport
- building effective working relationships
- listening
- questioning
- assertiveness.

In the work environment Interpersonal skills often overlap with technical/ procedural skills such as with performance management, where a manager needs the procedural skills of completing the processes and documentation effectively, but also needs appropriate interpersonal skills when conducting performance reviews.

We can summarize the outcome-based design process, so far, as being:

1 Identify the required outcomes through some form of training needs analysis (TNA):
   - formal/informal TNA
   - use of knowledge and experience of self and/or others.
2 Identify the skills and knowledge needed to achieve the required outcomes:

   Skills
   - The performance of the required outcomes.
   - Any underpinning or generic skills needed and not currently held.

   Knowledge
   - Technical or procedural knowledge to support the skills.
   - Any necessary background or theoretical knowledge.

Once you have identified the knowledge and skills that the learners need to help achieve the objective statements (and which they do not already have) you can move on to the next stages of the process which relate to identifying the most appropriate methods of providing the required knowledge and skills.

CHAPTER 3

Choosing the Methods

From the overall design processes described in the last chapter, you will now have your objective statements relating to what the learners will be able to do as a result of the training, and a list of the knowledge and skills needed to enable these objectives to be met. You are now in the position of identifying the most appropriate training methods to provide the necessary knowledge and skills. Towards the end of this chapter you will see where activity-based training fits into the scheme of these things.

METHODS FOR SKILLS

Training is all about learning and applying new skills, and in this way changing behaviour. Most training therefore should be skills based rather than knowledge based and the learning of those skills should take place as much as possible by *practising* them in one forum or another. If there is associated knowledge to be learned as well, this should be done beforehand so that the relevant knowledge can be applied or demonstrated during the skills practice. For the purposes of this book, I am using the classroom as the main forum for practising the required skills.

In my book *Participative Training Skills* I go into some detail about many of the training methods you can use to facilitate the learning of skills. It describes what the methods are and how to prepare for and deliver each of them. I will only touch here on what the main skills-practice methods are and what they can best be used for, as Table 3.1 shows.

Degrees of realism

When choosing an appropriate method for skills practice, another consideration is whether or not the activity should be based on a realistic work situation, or far removed from it.

A useful rule of thumb is that for any technical and procedural skills, the skills-practice activities should be as close as possible to actual work situations.

For interpersonal skills and many of the personal skills, however, the activities should allow concentration on the *process* of carrying out the skills or

Table 3.1 Choosing the method – skills methods

NAME	DEFINITION	RELEVANT SKILLS
CASE STUDY	A method in which an historical background scenario, set of circumstances or situation (real, imaginary or a mixture of both), with any other relevant data, is given to participants in written form for them to analyse and then diagnose or solve a particular problem	Technical/procedural Personal
ROLE PLAY	A method in which the participants, usually individually, act out a given scenario with the aim of practising appropriate skills involving the face-to-face activities they have to perform at work. Participants usually act as themselves, although can also take on the role of someone else. (Can sometimes be used as a follow-up to a case study)	Interpersonal Technical/procedural
FISHBOWL	A method in which a small group of participants form an inner circle and carry out an activity whilst being watched by the rest of the group who form an outer circle around them. The outer group observe, make notes, and offer feedback on the skills and/or behaviours of the inner group members	Interpersonal General behaviours
TECHNIQUE PRACTICE	A method in which short exercises are set up to enable the practice of particular skills and techniques. (Particular communication skills for example)	Interpersonal Personal
SIMULATIONS	A method whereby the training is set up to match an actual working environment as closely as possible. (Can include Presentation Skills or Trainer Training where the participants are asked to deliver actual presentations or sessions)	Personal Interpersonal Technical/procedural

behaviours. For example, if the objectives relate to carrying out the correct procedures for dealing with an organization's policy (something like sickness absence or discipline procedures) then any case-study or role-play scenarios will need to be as realistic as possible.

If on the other hand the objectives relate to more generic skills such as the process of project planning, then the process can be applied as much to planning the decoration of a room in a house as a work-based project. Planning the decoration of a room would allow concentration on the process, without the risk of getting bogged down in any work-related content.

METHODS FOR KNOWLEDGE

This is where activity-based design begins to come to the fore.

Table 3.2 shows the main methods for facilitating the learning of knowledge. To some extent the methods show an historical development from the lecturing/presentation approach to training, through the later movement towards participative methods, to now the development of Accelerated Learning and activity-based methods.

Whilst different skills methods are appropriate for different types of skill, the knowledge methods can be used for almost any kind of knowledge.

A variety of methods is usually recommended for the delivery of knowledge. This is still true, but as more and more delegates are experiencing and enjoying the activity-based approach, it is suggested that a higher percentage of time is spent on these methods (the methods described in this book!).

CHOOSING THE
METHODS

Table 3.2 Knowledge methods

METHOD	DESCRIPTION
PRESENTATION	Trainer presents information to group usually using visual aids such as: • PowerPoint • overhead projector/slides • flipchart • video Can also include 'demonstration role play' where two or more trainers act out a scenario for participants to observe and make notes Usually time for audience question during or at the end of the presentation Possibly interspersed with questions from the presenter Sometimes known as 'Chalk and Talk' or 'Pour and Snore' Nowadays only acceptable in small doses
PARTICIPATION	Question-and-Answer method used as a basis for a session Small group exercises (syndicates or buzz groups) to: • answer questions • solve problems • discuss issues Answers usually written up on flipchart Follow-up review of results by trainer
ACTIVITY-BASED (Accelerated Learning)	Trainer facilitates learning through group activities: • active reading • card-sort • games and activity boards (See rest of book!)

As a rough guide, you might like to think about the kind of split shown in Figure 3.1.

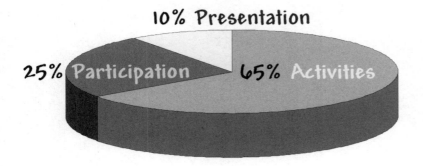

Figure 3.1   Percentages of method use

Please bear in mind though that the activity-based methods are mainly for the learning of *knowledge.* It is not recommended that they be used to replace any skills-practice exercises.

4

Materials, Equipment and Resources

In order to apply the activity-based training methods described in this book, you will need some raw materials and equipment to produce the finished training materials. I suspect that most would be available to you already. If not, the outlay of a relatively small financial investment may be required.

PC, PRINTER AND SOFTWARE

What can be done from this book can be done cheaply as long as you already have a PC or laptop and a printer. These are the only really expensive pieces of kit you will need. Furthermore, if you have a PC, chances are you will have Microsoft (MS) Word.

Everything described in this book can be done on MS Word. If you have any other drawing or publishing software, then that might help you cut a few corners or produce something a bit whizzier. But MS Word will do. I do urge you, however, to use as much of MS Word as you can. Experiment 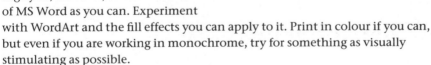 with WordArt and the fill effects you can apply to it. Print in colour if you can, but even if you are working in monochrome, try for something as visually stimulating as possible.

Use AutoShapes as well for any cards you make for the card-sort activities. Rectangles are fine, but ovals, hexagons, trapezoids and parallelograms will add that extra zest of shape to your cards.

LAMINATOR

Any cards you make for the card-sort activities will benefit immeasurably from being laminated. Some of the benefits to your cards are:

- You can re-use them time and again.
- They will not get tatty.
- Lamination makes them easier to stick to, and unstick from, any surface.
- The cards will stay flat and straight.
- They will look more professional.

Thanks to the upsurge of digital photography and home photo printing, laminators are now very inexpensive. The basic type of laminator requires your cards to be placed inside a pouch, which then is passed across heated rollers. The pouches too can now be picked up quite cheaply. An A4 size laminator will suffice for most purposes, although an A3 laminator would be worth considering for the extra things you can do with it.

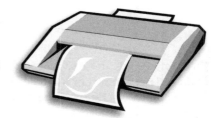

Another kind of laminator is a 'cold' type where your card is placed between two rolls of laminate film, and you wind it through like an old-fashioned washing mangle. The advantage of this type of laminator is that you can buy rolls of laminate up to 30 metres long, which works out cheaper than the equivalent number of pouches.

CARD

Coloured card or paper will be an essential for the card-sort activities. Card with a thickness of 120 or 160 gsm will work best, although coloured paper of 80 gsm will also be OK as long as it can be laminated.

Most of the time, A4 card will be all you need, although for some materials, such as game boards, coloured A3 paper or card will be needed.

CUTTING EQUIPMENT

Once you have laminated your cards, you will need to cut them out. For this, a paper trimmer or guillotine of some description will be useful. These are also now available in most stationery shops at reasonable cost. Trimmers are quicker than scissors, although you will also need scissors for any intricate cutting that might be needed. But if you can't get a trimmer, scissors will do the job fine.

ADHESIVES

If you are going to ask your participants to stick cards onto flipchart paper, and then stick the flipchart paper to the wall, you are going to need some form of adhesive.

Blu-tac and similar products are an obvious choice for this, but they do have their drawbacks. They can put a lot of weight onto the paper and the cards may fall off the flipchart sheet – and, more often than not, the flipchart sheet will fall off the wall. Alternatives to the tack materials are masking tape (low-tack to prevent pulling paint off the walls) or double-sided tape.

There is another, extremely cunning and secret solution to this problem, which I will now share with you. All you have to do is turn your flipchart sheet into 'magic paper'.

MAGIC PAPER

Magic paper has the seemingly miraculous quality of enabling cards to stick to it without any visible means of doing so. No tack, no tape.

It actually works by spraying some aerosol adhesive (like photo spray mount used to display pictures and posters for exhibitions) liberally to the paper a short while before you need to stick anything to it. If you put enough on and let it go tacky, it will easily take any number of cards and hold them there for days. There is often a look of astonishment on people's faces when they use magic paper for the first time without knowing the secret of its making.

All you have to ensure then is that you have the flipchart paper securely fixed to the wall by whatever other means you want to use.

OTHER PAPER

The chapters on card-sort exercises in this book usually talk about attaching the cards to flipchart paper. This is done for convenience, but is not always necessary or convenient. If you have limited wall space, you can use A3 or even A4 paper taped together and it can be made to fit any kind of space you may have. You can also use coloured paper instead of red, amber and green circles for your Traffic Light displays. Figure 4.1 shows some options.

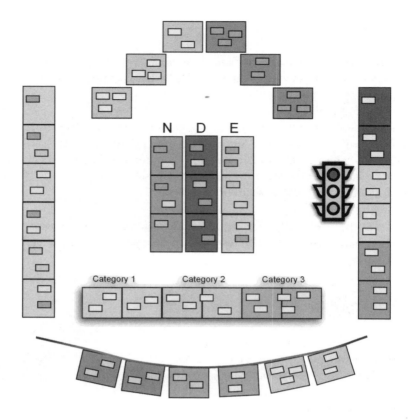

Figure 4.1   Magic paper – hanging options

POWERPOINT

One other resource I would like to mention briefly at this stage is PowerPoint. Of course you will need a projector and laptop (or dedicated PC) in order to use it, which will not be possible for everyone. Some of you may use PowerPoint in your sessions however, and might want to use it alongside some of the activity-based methods from this book. It is the *style* of PowerPoint that I would like to discuss here.

The methods in this book, and all the card-sort and game materials, should help to promote a relaxed environment and provide visual stimulation through colour and shape and so on, as has been mentioned earlier. Many PowerPoint presentations, unfortunately, do not complement this approach. A typical 'death by PowerPoint' presentation will be made up of slides chock-a-block with bullet points in text of a size that requires people at the back to have binoculars to read it.

There are many visual enhancements now available very cheaply through clip art CDs and free images from the Microsoft Office website. It always surprises me how little use is made of these. I recall someone saying once, quite dismissively, that clip art in PowerPoint was 'unprofessional'. I imagine that this person would also call many PowerPoint presentations 'professional' even though (or maybe because) they are dull lifeless and unimaginative.

Just to illustrate the point, I would like to show you a couple of 'before and after' PowerPoint slides. Unfortunately no animation is possible on the printed page, but please imagine the animation shown on all the slides whereby each bullet point or image appears one after the other, either dissolving or zooming in or suchlike.

The first 'before and after slides' (Figures 4.2 and 4.3) both cover the information often asked of people during the early 'group introductions' stage of a course.

Some introductions

- NAME/WHERE YOU WORK
- THE TRAINING YOU DO
- THE TRAINING METHODS/TECHNIQUES YOU USE
- ANY PREVIOUS TRAINER-TRAINING YOU HAVE HAD
- WHAT YOU HOPE TO GAIN FROM THIS EVENT
- ANY CONCERNS ABOUT THE WEEK AHEAD

Figure 4.2   Introductions – bullet points

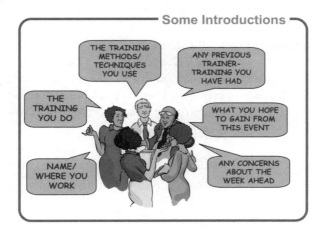

Figure 4.3   Introductions – illustrated

The second pair of slides (Figures 4.4 and 4.5) covers the setting of 'ground rules' also often carried out at the start of courses.

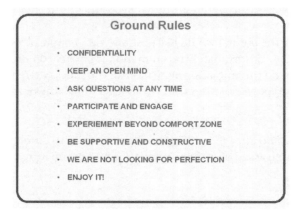

Figure 4.4   Ground rules – bullet points

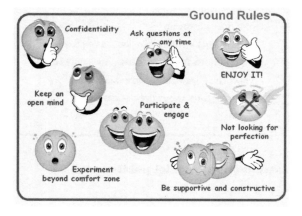

Figure 4.5   Ground rules – illustrated

As far as visual stimulation and establishing a relaxed environment for effective learning are concerned, you may agree that the usual bullet point approach can be improved upon, even if the alternative slides above are not to your particular taste. But I know which ones I prefer!

Part 2
Active Reading Materials

Sabotage

HOW IT WORKS

1   You ask people in pairs or small groups to examine a handout or some written material in order to find a number of errors contained within it.
2   People find and correct the errors, ending up with complete and accurate handouts.
3   You run through the errors and describe the corrections that should have been made.
4   You review the key messages that have been learned about the subject matter.

WHY IT WORKS

As a method, Sabotage is in tune with peoples' great ability to find mistakes and minor errors, no matter how small, in any kind of reading matter.

As trainers, we have probably all encountered the delegates who seem to take great pleasure in pointing out typos and any other kinds of minor discrepancy.

Sabotage makes the most of this ability to find faults, and provides people with some deliberate faults to find.

PURPOSE AND PRINCIPLES

Sabotage is a good way of getting people to read handouts or written material. Not only does it help people get a feel for the subject matter, it also helps the retention of the key points. It is also a more engaging alternative to the straightforward presentation of information on slides or flipchart.

PREPARATION

1   Choose some information that's covered in your training and that will be suitable for the Sabotage approach. Suitable information could be, for example:

    •   information that may be covered on two or three PowerPoint or overhead projector slides;
    •   information that is usually presented on a flipchart;
    •   information that is usually contained in a fairly brief handout (no more than four sides of A4).

2   On a PC, either type up or cut and paste the information and produce until you have a good 'un-sabotaged' copy that can be issued in handout form. Save this, then save it again as the copy that you are going to sabotage.

3   Change a number of items on your sabotage copy to make them incorrect in some way – but ensure that they can be easily amended or overwritten manually with a pen after being printed as handouts. (Alternatively have a set of correct handouts printed to issue after the activity.)

4   Make sure the errors relate to useful items of information. The errors are likely to be remembered more than the correct elements of the sabotaged handout, so make the things that will be remembered worth remembering.

5   Print sufficient copies of the handouts (sabotaged and un-sabotaged as needed). If people are going to keep their own corrected handout then you will need one per person. If you are going to issue fresh, correct handouts after the activity you may only need enough sabotaged copies for two or three people to examine and correct as a small group exercise.

RUNNING THE ACTIVITY

Briefing

You can introduce the activity with a form of words similar to that given in Figure A1.1.

SABOTAGE

You are employees of a company that is just about to launch an internal marketing and training campaign about personal power. This includes providing some information on how to receive feedback from others effectively. You have had a few trial copies of some leaflets produced, which give people some background information on receiving feedback.

You have received the first of the leaflets back from the printers, and to your horror you discover that they have been SABOTAGED! It appears that someone has changed some of the words and meanings of the information so that it is now totally misleading.

Corrected versions of the leaflets will be needed in around 10 minutes in order for them to be shown to the project sponsor.

Your task therefore is to identify – and make good – the sabotaged elements of the leaflet. You have 10 minutes to check through the leaflet and correct the errors.

Figure A1.1   Sabotage – briefing scenario

You can tell them how many errors there are to find if you wish, or you can wait until the review and ask the groups how many errors they have found, and see if there are any differences.

You can either provide a briefing orally, or issue the briefing in written form. If you plan to issue the instructions in writing, it is always a good idea to test out a first draft with a colleague to check that the instructions are clear.

Monitoring

This is usually an activity that works best with two or three people working through the sabotaged handouts. If you divide a larger group up into smaller groups but keep everyone in the same room, you will be able to listen in to their discussion and hear whether or not they are finding the intended errors.

Sometimes, depending on the material, participants may think that they have found an error, but in fact the piece of information is correct. It can be worthwhile listening out for misconceptions like this that you can discuss in the review.

Reviewing

Once the groups have examined the sabotaged handout, an effective way to review their findings is to ask each group to describe the errors they have found, and what they have replaced them with.

Ask the first group to describe the first error they discovered, nearest to the beginning of the document, and what they amended it to. Ask any other group to declare if they found an error before this on the document. Then ask the second group to describe the next error on the handout and their amendment, and so on until all the errors and their correct amendments have been identified.

Depending on the number of errors you have and where they are placed in the handout, you could review them on a paragraph-by-paragraph basis, whereby each group describes the errors and their amendments for a whole paragraph or section.

Check that their corrections are appropriate as the review progresses, and discuss any misconceptions or other issues raised. If any groups missed an error, make sure that they know what it is, why it is wrong and what it should be before you conclude the session.

If anyone has to amend their corrections on the sabotaged handouts, their copies of the handout could get rather messy. To rectify this, keep a supply of un-sabotaged handouts ready to issue if necessary.

You can see an example of a sabotaged handout in Figure A1.2. You may wish to try it for yourself and identify the sabotaged information. A correct handout is shown in Figure A1.3.

RECEIVING FEEDBACK: GUIDELINES	

Try to identify the positives/negatives of your performance for yourself, and try to:
        – overstate the negatives
        – understate the positives
        – and vice versa.
Do not be prepared to discuss your performance openly and honestly.	

Accept that the person giving the feedback is trying to **hurt you**, and criticize and blame you.	
When being given feedback on your performance:	
• **Listen** to what is being said. Try not to let an emotionol reoction get in the way. • **Note** (mentally) any questions or valid disagreements • **Clarify** any information/comments you are uncertain about by asking questions and/or paraphrasing what you thought you heard. • **Consider** ignoring what you have heard before deciding what to do with the feedback.	**Aim to demonstrate:** • defensiveness • making excuses • rationalizing • blaming someone/something else. It is OK to **explain** the thought process/intentions behind your actions (whilst accepting that the results may not have been what you hoped for). Treat the feedback as judgement, not-information.
Decide what to do with the feedback (in whole or in part). Options:	
Accept You agree with the feedback, and don't plan to modify your approach in the future.	**Reject** After due consideration, you agree with the feedback and do not plan to modify your approach in the future.
Check You delay your final decision to accept or reject and check out the feedback with another person first.	**Repeat** You delay your final decision until you have repeated the performance, and received no further feedback.

Figure A1.2   Sabotage – sabotaged guidelines

EXAMPLE OF USE

Sabotage has been used in management training as part of a session on assertiveness. Definitions of assertiveness, aggression and passivity were 'sabotaged' as were various pieces of information relating to human rights. The information the handout covered was used as an introduction to the subject, and further exercises and activities followed it.

In the assertiveness Sabotage activity ten pieces of information were sabotaged, and the groups were told this beforehand. Although they knew this, some groups still occasionally insisted there were either 9 or 11!

Some groups would overlook some of the sabotaged items, or miss something that was sabotaged, and state instead some information that actually wasn't sabotaged. As the designer of this Sabotage activity I was quite happy to see some groups get some answers wrong occasionally. It proved that the activity was not too easy to complete and that they still had to think about the information with which they were presented.

RECEIVING FEEDBACK: GUIDELINES	

Try to identify the positives/negatives of your performance for yourself, and try **not** to:
          – overstate the negatives
          – understate the positives
          – and vice versa.
~~Do not~~ Be prepared to discuss your performance openly and honestly.	

Accept that the person giving the feedback is trying to **help** you, not criticize or blame you.	
When being given feedback on your performance:	
• **Listen** to what is being said. Try not to let an emotion**al** reaction get in the way. • **Note** (mentally) any questions or valid disagreements • **Clarify** any information/ comments you are uncertain about by asking questions and/or paraphrasing what you thought you heard. • **Consider** ~~ignoring~~ what you have heard before deciding what to do with the feedback.	~~Aim to demonstrate~~: **Avoid**: • defensiveness • making excuses • rationalizing • blaming someone/something else. It is OK to **explain** the thought process/ intentions behind your actions (whilst accepting that the results may not have been what you hoped for). Treat the feedback as ~~judgement, not information~~ **information not judgement**.
Decide what to do with the feedback (in whole or in part). Options:	
Accept You agree with the feedback, and ~~don't~~ plan to modify your approach in the future.	**Reject** After due consideration, you **dis**agree with the feedback and do not plan to modify your approach in the future.
Check You delay your final decision to accept or reject and check out the feedback with another person first.	**Repeat** You delay your final decision until you have repeated the performance, and received ~~no~~ further feedback.

Figure A1.3   Sabotage – amended guidelines

SUMMARY

HOW IT WORKS	**Participants**
	• In pairs or small groups
	• Examine a written handout to find errors
	• When they find them, make corrections
	Trainer
	• Run through errors
	• Identify proper corrections
	• Review key learning points
WHY IT WORKS	• In tune with people's ability to find faults
	• Provides deliberate faults to find
PURPOSE and PRINCIPLES	• Encourage reading and understanding of written materials
	• Get general 'feel' for subject matter
	• Help retention of key points
	• More engaging than straight presentation
PREPARATION	**Find suitable content**
	• Existing PowerPoint or OHP slides/flipchart presentation/ written handouts (up to four sides of A4)
	Produce on PC
	• Un-sabotaged copy
	• Sabotaged copy (changes to be easy to correct and important pieces of information
	• Written briefing (optional) of scenario and instructions
	•
	Print copies
	• Sabotaged – one per person or one per group
	• Un-sabotaged – one per person as final handout
RUNNING	**Briefing**
	• Introduce with scenario. Written or verbal
	Monitoring
	Listen to discussions
	• Are the groups correctly identifying errors?
	• Any misconceptions?
	• Note any points for review
	Reviewing
	• Groups to state answers in turn
	• Check if others agree and explore any misconceptions
	• Bring in own observations from monitoring if necessary
	• Ensure all participants are clear on final answers and reasons why

Missing Bullet Points

HOW IT WORKS

1   You give people a handout, but with empty spaces wherever any groups of bullet points should be.
2   You then give them a sheet of paper on which all the groups of bullet points have been printed (in a random sequence).
3   The participants' task is then to cut out the bullet points, and stick them into the correct spaces on the handout with glue.
4   You review their results and issue the complete handout.

WHY IT WORKS

Missing Bullet Points allows people to see the detailed content of written materials, and how it fits in a particular context. Participants must read the bullet points *and* the relevant text if they are to stick the bullet points into the correct space.

Within this activity there is movement and a range of different things to be done: reading, cutting out, sticking, and so on. In this respect the Missing Bullet

Points activity could also be used as a team-working exercise with people being allocated roles of cutting out the bullet points, applying the glue, sticking the bullet points into the relevant spaces and so on.

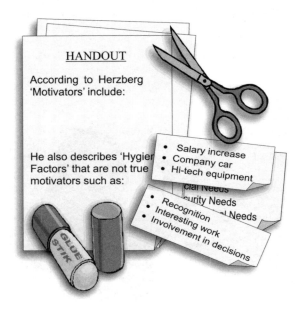

PURPOSE AND PRINCIPLES

The Missing Bullet Points approach is a good way of getting people to get a feel for the content of handouts and written material around five to ten pages in length.

The activity works on similar principles to a jigsaw puzzle, but using selected words (bullet points) instead of pieces of a picture. It could also be compared to making up a scrapbook.

You can use Missing Bullet Points as an individual or as a small group activity. Most often, however, it works best as a small group activity, which allows for more discussion and debate.

PREPARATION

1   Choose a handout or a series of PowerPoint slides etc that contain a reasonable number of bullet points (between six and ten sets). If you are using material other than an existing handout, cut and paste or type up the material until you have a final product that can be issued as a handout – with a sufficient number of bullet points of course!

2   Edit the handout to cut the bullet points, but keep the same amount of blank space where the bullet points used to be on the page. In fact, it is best to give a little more space to ensure that the cut-out bullet points can be stuck back in without covering up any of the remaining text.

Make sure you keep the introductory text *prior* to the bullet points in place to provide the necessary clue as to what bullet points should follow. See Figure A2.1 for an example.

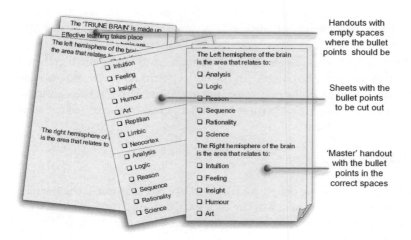

Figure A2.1   Missing Bullet Points – pages

3   Electronically paste the bullet points *only* onto a new page and mix up the sequence so that they are in a different order than in the original handout.
4   Depending on how much 'play' you want people to have, you could give them the sheet of paper with all the bullet points for them to cut out and stick, or you could give them pre-cut bullet points which just have to be stuck. (Glue-sticks and possibly scissors will therefore need to be made available for people to use.)
5   Print off as many copies of the following as you need, depending on how you want to run the activity (see below):

•   handouts with bullet points *removed*
•   sheets of bullet points (or sets if pre-cut)
•   original handouts that *include* the bullet points.

If your original written material does not contain many sets of bullet points, it is usually quite straightforward to turn a normal paragraph of text into an introductory sentence followed by the remaining sentences turned into bullet points.

A quick example of how a Missing Bullet Points page might look is shown in Figures A2.3 and A2.4.

RUNNING THE ACTIVITY

This activity can be run as an individual or small group activity where *each person* has a handout with the bullet points removed, and a sheet/set of the mixed-up bullet points to stick into the relevant spaces. They can work individually or together to complete the task and can then keep their final products as their own handouts

Missing Bullet Points can also be run as a team effort where small groups of people are given *one* handout with the bullet points removed and *one* sheet/set of the mixed up bullet points for sticking. When this has been accurately completed, handouts that include the bullet points can be issued to everyone on an individual basis.

Briefing

A good way of briefing people for this kind of exercise is to tell them what the subject matter or topic is at the very start, but not to give too much away about how the session will run until you launch into the scenario of the kind suggested below. As with Activity 1, Sabotage, you can issue your briefing and instructions orally or in writing (see Figure A2.2). You can thus introduce the activity with a form of words something like those in the example.

PRINTING CRISIS

You have just written an important information sheet on group development for distribution to all team leaders. It has just come back from the printers for proof reading, and they have made a horrible mistake.

Their new computerized system seems to have cut out all the bullet points from their proper places, and printed them in a random order on separate sheets of paper.

Therefore, your task is to identify where the bullet points should go, and stick them in their correct positions. Time is of the essence, and you have 15 minutes to produce acceptable copies for distribution.

Figure A2.2   Missing Bullet Points – briefing scenario

Monitoring

Once the groups have been briefed and are under way with the activity, you will need to consider the amount of monitoring and intervening that you will do. You can either make the necessary interventions to help people get back on track if they veer from the point at any time, or you can wait.

In most cases it will be preferable to wait. If a group puts a set of bullet points in the wrong space, there is a good chance that they will realize that something has gone wrong later in the activity when they are likely to have another set of bullet points that do not seem to fit anywhere! This will mean that they have to re-check their previous work.

Reviewing

If you run this as an activity with three or four groups in the same room, or in syndicate rooms, you can review this activity with all the groups present. Review their results by asking each in turn to state what bullet points they have put in place.

You would therefore ask the first group to state the bullet points they have placed in the first empty space in the handout. Next, the second group state what they have placed in the second empty space, then the third group with the third space, and so on, until you have worked through the whole handout.

If there are any inaccuracies or misconceptions, you can ask the groups who have got the correct answers to explain their thoughts to the group(s) who have not.

You can run the activity purely as a way of helping people become familiar with the written material, or when used with the team approach described above, you can use it as a team-working or leadership activity and review it along the lines of:

*   how well the group worked as a team to complete the task;
*   how well the leader got the task done through the team.

EXAMPLE OF USE

The Missing Bullet Points method has been used on a number of different types of course. It has been used for topics such as the management skills of planning and monitoring performance, the theory of group development and the manager's role in implementing new policies.

The method can of course be used for almost any kind of knowledge, as long as you have some accompanying text that can be turned into bullet points.

Experience has shown that, if you are using this as a straight method to help learn the scope and content of some text, it is best to pre-cut the bullet points. If participants are given a set to cut out, it invariably means that the person who does the cutting out does not contribute very much to the discussions on where the bullet points should fit, which is the main point of the activity. If the method is used as a team-working activity, however, it is best to have the cutting out as a task for a member of the team to do. Figures A2.3 and A2.4 show a pages from the Missing Bullet Points activity on the subject of group development as mentioned above.

GROUP DEVELOPMENT

The following theory of group development describes the stages that a group can grow through from the time of its first formation. This section will also cover the action you, as a trainer, can take in regard to each stage to help build the right kind of learning climate. As the action to take is described, you will be able to recognize how this theory has certain similarities with Maslow's Hierarchy of Needs model.

There are four main stages that a group can go through as it develops. Tuckman called them Forming, Storming, Norming and Performing.

Another way of naming the stages highlights the similarities of group development to people's development through the stages of life, that is: Childhood, Adolescence, Young Adulthood and Maturity.

The Forming /Childhood stage

Characteristics and behaviours of this stage

Actions you can take as the trainer during the Forming/Childhood stage

The Storming/Adolescence stage

Characteristics and behaviours of this stage

Actions you can take as the trainer during the Storming/Adolescence stage

---

Figure A2.3   Group Development – missing bullets

BULLET POINTS

- Boundaries begin to be explored and the limits of acceptable behaviour are tested out.
- It is the stage of rebelliousness by action or inaction.
- Behavioural changes might be in evidence, such as quiet people becoming loud and vice versa.
- Suggestions about tackling tasks will be rejected.
- Any conflicts between group members will become apparent (or they might all join forces to attack you instead).
- Complaints about the course content, the exercises, and the training material are likely to be vocalized at this stage.

- People feel most vulnerable, and wonder where they will fit in.
- Fear and suspicion about the unknown run high.
- There is a deep-felt need for guidance, direction and structure.
- Cliques may form.
- People will prefer to be told what to do rather than be given difficult or too many choices.
- People will be concerned about what the other group members will be like (and what the trainers will be like).
- Defensive behaviours such as withdrawal or brashness will be in evidence.

- Ignore it and wait for it to pass.
- Find out the cause of the perceived problem, raise the issue with the group, and try to resolve it.
- Give the trainees the opportunity to express their dissatisfaction without any judgements, rationalizations, excuses or arguments on your part.
- Be prepared to mix socially with the group to build rapport and avoid an 'us and them' situation. (If socializing is not your forte, try to mix during an occasional coffee break.)

- Supply clear information about the course, its objectives, the timetable and the methods.
- Setting ground rules.
- Make sure that the first one or two exercises are not too difficult and do not involve high levels of risk.
- Make doubly sure that briefings are clearly understood
- Encourage individuals to participate without putting them under too much pressure to do so.

Figure A2.4   Group Development – bullets only

SUMMARY

HOW IT WORKS	**Trainer**
	• Issue handout with empty spaces where bullet points should be
	• Issue sheet of paper with bullet points only printed in random order (or issue set of pre-cut bullet points)
	• Issue glue sticks (one or more per group) and scissors if required
	Groups
	• Cut out bullet points and stick into correct spaces
	• Trainer
	• Review results
	• Issue full handout (complete with bullet points)
WHY IT WORKS	• Promotes reading of written material
	• Text and bullet points need to be read in order to complete the activity
	• Includes movement/action/discussion/touch and manipulation
	• People work together as a team
PURPOSE AND PRINCIPLES	• Provision of broad understanding of written material (5–10 pages)
	• Similar to completing a jigsaw puzzle or a scrapbook
	• Activity for individuals or small groups (small groups better for more discussion)
PREPARATION	**Find suitable material**
	• Existing handouts or PowerPoint slides with between 6 and 10 sets of bullet points
	• Rewrite if necessary to add sets of bullet points
	Edit material on PC
	• Cut out bullet points and leave sufficient blank spaces
	• Keep words immediately prior to bullet points to provide context and clues
	• Paste bullet points only on new page in random order
	Print
	• Handouts with bullet points removed
	• Sheets of bullet points in random order (pre-cut if required)
	• Produce and print
	• Written briefing and instructions if required
RUNNING	**Briefing**
	• Explain purpose of activity and provide written or verbal instructions
	Monitoring
	• Can intervene to assist if necessary
	• Usually preferable to wait (groups often identify errors for themselves)
	Reviewing
	• Each group in turn to describe where they have placed their bullet points (one group/one set of bullet points at a time)
	• Check if other groups agree
	• Discuss misconceptions and rationales
	• Summarize and confirm correct placements and key learning points
	• Review effectiveness of teamwork if required

Sticky Tips

HOW IT WORKS

1   You issue teams with a complex or multi-page form, with a set of tips or guidance (in random order) on how to complete each section of it.
2   You ask the groups to stick the tips/guidance onto what they think is the relevant section of the form.
3   You run through their results and review the accuracy of their placing, discussing any issues or questions that may arise.
4   You issue handouts of the document with the tips pasted electronically.

WHY IT WORKS

If you have ever run a session that involves explaining how a form or document should be completed, you may have had the experience of participants wanting to know everything at once, or wanting to discuss their own experiences or issues. When this type of situation arises you can quickly find yourself bogged down in the detail, and having to deal with a whole string of 'But what if …?' questions. Sticky Tips can do a lot to prevent this.

Furthermore, not only can Sticky Tips help people become familiar with certain forms and documents, it can also allow for any misconceptions about any sections of the document to become apparent and be dealt with.

Sticky Tips also works well as an activity to introduce people to the document in question and thus as a forerunner to a follow-up case study, for example, through which the delegates will be able to practise the actual completion of the document.

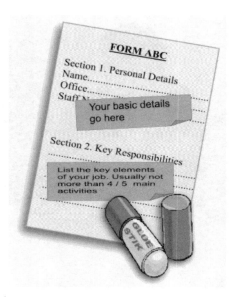

PURPOSE AND PRINCIPLES

Within organizations there are likely to be long or complex internal forms and documents with various sections to complete, such as appraisal documents and internal job application forms. In some organizations, employees need to deal with complex forms that are sent out to the public.

Working in a similar way to Missing Bullet Points (Activity 2), Sticky Tips enables the guidance on how to complete or process the forms to be matched and stuck directly to the appropriate sections of the form. These can then be kept as a permanent reference document.

PREPARATION

Using the Sticky Tips method requires you to draft the instructions or information about each particular section of the document onto slips of paper, somewhere between one and three inches wide.

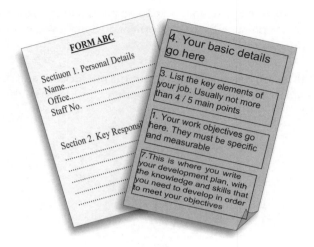

Some forms may already have guidance (tips) on how to fill them in which you can use as a reference point. You should of course take out any direct references to any particular sections of the form.

It can be a good idea to number the slips of paper in a different sequence to how they appear on the form. This will help when reviewing the activity. You could also give them a coloured or grey background, or print them on coloured paper so that they will stand out when stuck onto the form.

If possible, try to avoid writing out too much information on each slip of paper. The objective of this activity should be more about enabling the delegates to become generally familiar with the overall content and scope of the documentation.

Cut and paste the instructions onto an electronic copy of the document if you can, so that you can use this as a master document and handout. Print one or more master copies depending on how you want to run the activity.

If this is done as a small-group activity, have a sufficient number of master copies ready to issue one to everybody. If it is run as an individual activity, people could keep their own work or you could issue them with master copies as well – which will probably be neater.

RUNNING THE ACTIVITY

Briefing

As with any exercise and activity, you will need to introduce the topic and explain what is going to happen. The purpose and limitations of the exercise should also be explained. You might need to explain that this activity will be an introductory overview, and that the form or document will be looked at in greater depth afterwards.

Issue the blank forms, the slips of paper with the instructions and some glue sticks. Ask people to stick the slips over what they consider to be the correct section of the form.

Monitoring

If your participants are all in the same room, you can wander around to look and listen as to what is going on. As was the case with the monitoring of Missing Bullet Points, you will need to decide whether or not to intervene if it appears that an individual or a group is heading off track.

Also as was the case with Missing Bullet Points, it will probably be better to wait before intervening. If one tip is stuck onto an incorrect section of the form, this may be realized later when the correct tip will not seem to fit in any of the remaining sections. In any event, you may want to leave any incorrect tip placements until you deal with them in the review.

Reviewing

When the activity has been completed, review it by asking the groups or individuals to state the number on the slip that they have stuck onto each section (you may remember it was suggested that you number each slip at the preparation stage). You can then compare this to your 'master copy'.

It is at this point that you can discuss any misplaced slips or misconceptions about the nature of the documents. Ensure that everyone is aware of the actual meaning and requirements of the document before you move on to anything else.

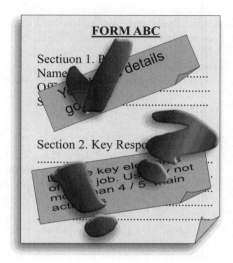

If you run this activity as a small group exercise, you could add a slightly competitive element to it with a small prize awarded for the most accurate or fastest completion. (Not recommended if run as an individual activity as there can be more dangers to introducing competition between individuals.)

EXAMPLE OF USE

Sticky Tips has been used successfully in the area of performance management training, where the tips related to a staff performance agreement and appraisal form that was split into several sections.

The activity showed up a number of misconceptions that people had about the completion of the form, especially in the areas of how much information to include. As an example of this, one section of the form asked for people to list the key knowledge and skills required for their job role. The 'tip' said that this meant the knowledge and skills that *anyone* would need were they to be doing that job. Many participants were under the misapprehension that they had to write the knowledge and skills they needed *to develop*. In fact, there was another separate section of the form to record development needs.

On this course, the Sticky Tips activity was followed by an in-depth case study that allowed the participants to complete the form and other performance management processes correctly.

SUMMARY

HOW IT WORKS	**Trainer** • Issue groups with complex and/or multi-page form • Issue slips of paper which show 'tips' on purpose and completion of each section of the form • Issue glue sticks (one or more per group) **Groups** • Stick the tips onto what they think is the correct section of the form **Trainer** • Review results • Issue handout with tips pasted onto form electronically
WHY IT WORKS	• Prevents getting bogged down in too much detail too soon • Effective introduction to a complex document and a possible forerunner to a case study or further information • Allows any misconceptions to be highlighted • People work together as a team
PURPOSE AND PRINCIPLES	• Enables written guidance to be matched directly to the document • Similar to completing a jigsaw puzzle or a scrapbook (like Missing Bullet Points) • Activity for individuals or small groups (small groups better for more discussion)
PREPARATION	• Use or edit existing guidance notes if available • Draft own guidance notes if necessary • Avoid putting too much information on each slip and information that would make correct location too obvious • Number each slip (differently to any section numbers used on the form) • Print on paper of different colour to the form, or on a grey or coloured background • Copy and paste tips electronically onto the form and print as final handout
RUNNING	**Briefing** • Explain purpose of activity and any follow-up activity • Give written or verbal instructions on what is to be done **Monitoring** • Can intervene to assist if necessary • Usually preferable to wait (groups often identify errors for themselves) **Reviewing** • Each group in turn state the slip number they have stuck to each section of the form – one at a time • Discuss misconceptions and rationales • Summarize and confirm correct placements and key learning points

Info Hunt

HOW IT WORKS

1   You give people (small groups or individually) a handout or other written material (such as guidance notes, policy documents or instruction manuals).

2   You also issue a written questionnaire with boxes or spaces in which the answers can be written.

3   You ask participants to work through the written material and complete the questionnaire as they go along.

4   On completion, you run through the answers, review the results and issue handouts to all.

WHY IT WORKS

The Info Hunt activity promotes the reading of a relatively long document in order for people to become familiar with its content. People have to read and search through all of the material to hunt out the information needed to answer the questions.

It is a little like giving people a questionnaire to complete as a test of their knowledge of the subject matter, but providing them with all the answers on a separate document as well.

Info Hunt works because it gives a reason for reading a document. It also works because there can be a sense of achievement at the end of it, and if required, you can add an element of competition.

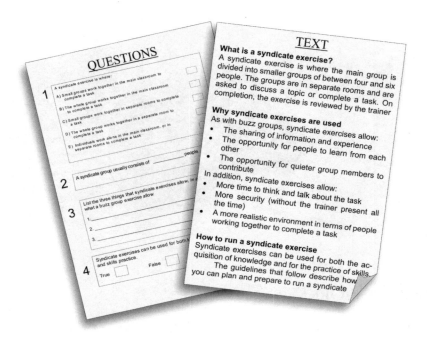

PURPOSE AND PRINCIPLES

Info Hunt is a good way of getting people to become familiar with a relatively large amount of written material – up to about 15 pages long. It works particularly well with information on policies or procedures.

It is also useful for helping people remember key items of information, once there has been a mental connection made between the question and the answer.

PREPARATION

For this activity you will need an appropriate piece of written material that your learners need to become familiar with. It should be quite lengthy to allow you the scope to devise a sufficient number of questions, say 20 to 30.

It is important to ensure that the questions follow the same sequence as the content of the written materials so that people are *not* required to search back and forth through the material. This would greatly increase the time needed for the activity and would probably be frustrating for the participants.

Devising the questions

The most effective types of question for this activity are a mixture of:

- true/false
- short answer
- multiple choice.

These questions will be drafted in the knowledge that people will have the answers in front of them within the written material that they have been given. The questions are therefore not designed to test learners' knowledge or memory. They are to help them realize the scope and coverage of the written information in front of them.

True/false

This type of question is produced by simply taking a statement from the text, and reproducing it (possibly with minor amendments) as a true statement, or changing it in order to make it false. When drafting true/false questions, try to ensure that each statement represents an important piece of information. And avoid making the statements too obviously true or false.

Syndicate exercises can be used for both knowledge acquisition and skills practice.

True ☐   False ☐

Figure A4.1   Example of a true/false question

Some other tips when drafting true/false questions:

- Include only one significant idea in each statement.
- Word the statement so that it is unequivocally true or false.
- Keep the statements short and use simple language.

- Avoid double negatives.
- Emphasize negative words in some way so that they are not overlooked (e.g. NOT, *never*, <u>no</u>).
- Use an approximately equal number of true and false questions throughout the questionnaire.

An example is given in Figure A4.1.

Short answer

Short-answer questions can be drafted in two main styles.

The first style is a straightforward question accompanied by a box in which the answer can be written. Figure A4.2 is an example.

Q: A syndicate group usually consists of how many people?

A:

Figure A4.2   Example of a short-answer question (1)

Questions of this style should require just a single word or a single sentence to constitute the answer.

Make sure the box you draw is big enough for people to write the required answer, but small enough so as not to promote the writing of an essay.

The second type of short-answer question is where people are asked to fill-in the blanks of a given sentence or statement. An example is given in Figure A4.3.

A syndicate group usually consists of _____ people.

Figure A4.3   Example of a short-answer question (2)

For this style of short-answer question the blank should be placed at or near the end of the sentence. It should also be a key word that is omitted from the sentence, as this will aid its retention in people's memory. People should not be asked to supply words like 'and' or 'the'.

Other tips for writing short-answer questions of either style are to phrase the question or statement so that only a single brief answer is possible, which is not always easy. See Figure A4.4 for an example.

> Syndicate exercises can be used for _____

Figure A4.4   Example of a wide question

This invites a whole host of answers that could be deemed as being correct, even though it may not relate to the information provided in the written material.

Also, make sure that all questions are short, concise and unambiguous.

You can ask multiple short-answer questions like the example in Figure A4.5.

> List the three things that syndicate exercises allow, in addition to what a buzz group exercise allows:
> 1.
> 2.
> 3.

Figure A4.5   Example of a multiple short-answer question

A type of multiple short-answer question to avoid is one that consists of one sentence with multiple spaces that can be confusing if the answers are not immediately obvious, such as in Figure A4.6.

> If _____ is _____then _____ must be _____

Figure A4.6   Example of a type of multiple question to avoid

Multiple choice

A multiple-choice question consists of a 'stem' which is the question, situation or problem, with several alternative answers for people to choose from. There will be one or more correct answers within the alternatives.

There are usually four or five alternatives for multiple-choice questions when there is just one correct answer. If there are numerous correct answers, you will need to have more incorrect alternatives (or 'distractors'). The incorrect alternatives should not be too obviously incorrect.

As with the other types of question, the multiple-choice question should relate to important items of information.

A difficulty some writers have is finding a sufficient number of viable alternatives as the distractors. Try to make them plausible so that people will need to read the written material in order to discover the correct ones.

An example of a good multiple-choice question is shown in Figure A4.7.

Some other tips about writing multiple-choice questions:

- The question or task given in the stem should be clearly understood by participants without their needing to read any of the alternative answers provided.
- Keep the question or task given in the stem clear and simple.
- Put as much of the wording as possible into the stem, so you do not repeat the same words in all of the alternatives.
- If you use a negative in the stem, make sure it is emphasized in some way as for true/false questions (e.g. NO, *never*, <u>not</u>).
- Make sure the intended answer is unquestionably correct or clearly best.
- Make sure all the alternatives are grammatically consistent with the stem, and each other.
- Make sure all the alternatives are consistent in their length and amount of detail. The length of the correct answer can often require more words than the distractors in order to make it unequivocally correct. If this happens, adjust the distractors to make them longer.

A syndicate exercise is where:
  a) Small groups work together in the main classroom to complete a task
  b) The whole group works together in the main classroom to complete a task
  c) Small groups work together in separate rooms to complete a task
  d) The whole group works together in a separate room to complete a task
  e) Individuals work alone in the main classroom, or in separate rooms to complete a task

---

Figure A4.7   Example of a multiple-choice question

An important element of running this activity is to ensure that the questions make sense, and that they allow people to respond with the correct answer easily once it has been found in the text. The best way to ensure this is to draft the questions and then test them out on friends or colleagues. This will also be useful in giving you an idea of how much time the activity will take.

RUNNING THE ACTIVITY

Briefing

For this activity you will need to introduce the topic and explain the process. Delegates will need to be clear that the questions in the questionnaire appear in the same sequence as the information in the main text. They could feel demoralized if they think they will need to search around the whole text to answer each question.

If you are using Info Hunt as a small group activity, still only issue one copy of the written material and questionnaire. This will promote a 'huddle' for discussion and interaction.

Monitoring

Due to the length of time that this activity can take, you might find that some groups steam through it more quickly than others. Keep your eyes and ears open as people work their way through the activity, and possibly provide some hints for any group or individual falling behind.

Fast-finishing groups can be asked to double-check some of their answers. If during your monitoring you have noticed one or two incorrect answers from a fast group, you can suggest that they check again in the relevant section of the text.

Reviewing

The review of this activity requires the answers to be given to the groups so they can see how accurate and successful they have been. You can do this in a number of ways, such as:

- issuing a copy of the questionnaire with the answers included, and taking further questions from the groups if necessary as they check their answers;
- issuing the answers as above and getting each group to score *another* group's answers, and then also taking questions as above;
- reading out the answers to each question yourself (this will allow discussion and clarification of any points if necessary);
- asking one group at a time to read out their answer to each question, and checking if the others have the same answer. You can then state the correct answer and discuss as necessary.

Once again, this is an activity you can make competitive by having a prize for the team with the highest number of correct answers, or the fastest finishers.

Example of use

This activity has been used for the training of groups of civil servants in the UK on the subject of answering parliamentary questions. It was carried out by three groups of around four people each.

The relevant guidance notes relating to the departmental procedures for answering parliamentary questions were printed from the department's intranet, and the questionnaire was devised around them. There were around 12 sides of intranet guidance when printed onto A4, and about 25 questions (some requiring multiple answers). The questions were a mixture of all the types mentioned above.

The activity worked in terms of meeting its objectives of enabling participants to become familiar with the content and scope of the intranet guidance, and also knowing where to look to find the relevant guidance when needed.

Although no prize was offered, there was still an inherent competitive element to the exercise that added a degree of energy and excitement during the completion time and especially when it came around to reading out the answers.

SUMMARY

HOW IT WORKS	**Trainer** • Issue a handout or other written material up to around 15 pages in length (one per group) • Issue a questionnaire with boxes or spaces for answers to be written **Groups** • Read the written material and complete the questionnaire as they go along **Trainer** • Run through the answers • Issue handout/written material to all individuals
WHY IT WORKS	• Promotes reading of a relatively long document • Participants have to hunt out the answers to the questions by reading the material • Sense of achievement at the end • Motivation through competitive element (whether intentional or not)
PURPOSE AND PRINCIPLES	• Provision of understanding of scope and coverage of written material (10–15 pages) • Assists recall of information • Most appropriate as small-group activity

PREPARATION	**Find suitable material**
	• Handout or other lengthy written material on policies, procedures etc.
	• Sufficient length for about 20–30 questions to be asked
	• Draft questionnaire
	• Questions to be in same sequence as written material
	• Types of question to use:
	  • true/false
	  • short answer
	  • multiple choice
	• Test out before using on live training event
	• Produce questionnaire with answers for review purposes and possible issue as handout

RUNNING	**Briefing** • Explain purpose of activity and provide written or verbal instructions • Point out that questions are in same sequence as text • Issue one copy of questionnaire and text per group of two or three people **Monitoring** • Check on slower/quicker groups • Can offer hints to slower group, and ask quicker groups to double check (especially if you notice any incorrect answers) **Reviewing options** • Issue questionnaire with answers included for groups to self-score or score another group's questionnaire • Read out the answers yourself and discuss as necessary • Ask one group at a time to read out their answer and check if other groups have same answer • Discuss and clarify any incorrect answers as necessary

Highlight Hierarchy

HOW IT WORKS

1 Issue the handout or written material that you want people to read.
2 Ask people individually to highlight what they think are the key points either using actual highlighter pens, or by circling or underlining with a pen or pencil.
3 Then, also individually, to note their top, say five to ten, key points.
4 Put people into small groups to compare ideas and reach a consensus view on the group's top five to ten points, with the option of writing these up on flipchart paper.
5 Review the top five to ten points and compare with the other groups' results.

WHY IT WORKS

A lot of written material contains many more words than just the essentials and sometimes key pieces of information can be overlooked. Furthermore, what is essential or important for one person may not be so essential or important for another. The Highlight Hierarchy activity can help to 'highlight' either or both of these principles.

PURPOSE AND PRINCIPLES

You can run Highlight Hierarchy as a straightforward way of getting people familiar with the relevant written material, and identifying the most important elements.

Highlight Hierarchy can also however be used as a communication exercise to identify the interpersonal skills used during the consensus-seeking part of the activity. If this is to be the main purpose, the learning achieved through the highlighting exercise should be considered as being of secondary concern.

PREPARATION

There is very little preparation required for this activity. Initially you need some written material that *does* convey some important items of information, or is somehow contentious.

If being used as a communication-skills exercise, the material should include issues involving people's beliefs and values and where there could be a range of different (but valid) opinions. A controversial magazine or newspaper article, or findings from an internal or external report, could provide the kind of material needed. Written material on equal opportunities and diversity issues can often provide content that pull upon individuals' belief and value systems.

From this point, you need:

- a copy of the material for each participant;
- sufficient numbers of highlighters or other pens or pencils;
- flipchart paper and possibly Blu-tac to stick it to a wall;
- flipchart pens.

RUNNING A STRAIGHTFORWARD ACTIVE-READING EXERCISE

Briefing

As usual, you will need to brief the group about the logistics of the activity and what people are asked to do.

You will need to inform people about where they should go if the second part of the activity is taking part in syndicate rooms. This element of the briefing should also let people know about the relevant timings for each part of the activity.

Before you divide the main group into smaller groups, ask them to ensure that at least one person is prepared to talk through their results at the end. From this point you will only need to issue the materials, and then start the individual part of the exercise.

Monitoring

Both forms of activity will require you to keep a watchful eye on the time when people are completing the reading/highlighting element. There are bound to be differences in the time it takes different people to read and highlight. If necessary, the quicker people could be asked to prioritize their key points, whilst the less quick people could skip that stage and contribute their ideas only at the group consensus stage.

Review

If just the reading and highlighting element of the activity is required, the review of the activity will be to ask each group to present their 'top five to ten' and see how they compare with other groups' findings. Commonalities and differences can then be discussed. If necessary, you can step in with thoughts on any important points that may have been overlooked.

RUNNING IT AS A COMMUNICATION EXERCISE

Briefing

If the activity is more of a communication exercise, then you will not want to give too much away about what the actual purpose of the activity is. If people are too aware of the nature of this kind of activity, they are more likely to behave differently to normal. You can provide the same logistical information as for the straightforward active-reading exercise, but not too much more.

Monitoring

This kind of communication exercise requires a trainer to be present with each group as they work through the consensus-seeking process. Each trainer should observe, take notes, but not intervene in the group processes.

Bear in mind that if used as a communication exercise, the actual reaching of a consensus agreement is not the main purpose of the activity. It doesn't matter if a consensus agreement is reached or not. The communication processes used when trying to reach an agreement are the key elements to be reviewed.

Reviewing

The review of the communication exercise will be better conducted within each small group. People can then be asked to comment on their own and others' communication skills in areas such as:

- listening/letting others have their say
- interrupting/dominating
- seeking or blocking ideas
- supporting or attacking others.

Because of the potential emotional content of this kind of exercise, the trainer needs to facilitate the process carefully and sensitively.

EXAMPLE OF USE

Highlight Hierarchy and other forms of consensus-seeking activity are quite common in management and other interpersonal skills training. Because people are asked to identify their own 'top five' issues, for example, and determine their own ideas about priorities, there is a strong inclination to hold on tightly to these opinions. In the minds of some they become facts rather than opinions and there can be resentment if anyone challenges them.

The effect of the activity is strengthened or weakened by the content of the written material. The strongest texts involve issues that are highly value laden and may prompt the expression of deep-seated prejudices and fears. For most training purposes, there will be no need to go to these depths.

SUMMARY

HOW IT WORKS	**Trainer** • Issue a handout or other written material **Groups** • Individually read the written material and highlight/prioritize what they believe are the key points or issues (top five to ten) • Work in small groups of four to six people to agree a consensus top five to ten key points **Trainer** • Bring groups back together and review their results • Review communication process within groups during consensus stage (if appropriate)
WHY IT WORKS	• Can promote and highlight key points contained within written materials, so they are not overlooked • Can help establish that what is more important for one person may be less important for another
PURPOSE AND PRINCIPLES	• Can be used to highlight key items of information • Can be used as a communication exercise for feedback on interpersonal skills demonstrated
PREPARATION	• Use handout or other written material that contains some key points, and may also be relatively contentious • For the communication exercise, use written material that includes issues relating to people's beliefs and values (such as Equal Opportunities and Diversity) • Prepare written briefing and instructions if required • Provide highlighter pens if available
RUNNING	**Briefing** • Explain purpose of activity and provide written or verbal instructions (not too much detail on purpose if used as communication exercise) • Explain the logistics and timings • Divide into syndicate groups after individual element completed and dispatch to syndicate rooms **Monitoring** • Check on slower/quicker individual completion • Invite quicker individuals to begin prioritization/slower people can prioritize at group stage • If highlight only exercise – minimal monitoring needed • If communication exercise – monitor as much as possible but avoid intervening. Note any points to raise in review **Reviewing** • If highlight only – allow groups to present their results and discuss as necessary • If communication exercise – review and facilitate provision feedback on demonstration of individuals' communication skills (back in small groups for review)

Before and After

HOW IT WORKS

1   You issue a sheet with written questions or true/false statements relating to a topic for which there is associated reading material. In small groups or individually, people complete the sheet *before* reading the written material.
2   You then issue the written material for people to read, after which they put it to one side or return it to you.
3   You then ask people to answer the same questions etc. *after* they have read the material.
4   You review the results, paying particular attention to any differences.

WHY IT WORKS

This method enables people's reading to be more focused and concentrated. Like Info Hunt (Activity 4), it promotes reading with a purpose.

The *after* reading especially tunes people in to finding out whether or not their original answers were correct. It therefore avoids a common problem with reading, which is just skimming the content and reading with no real desire to identify any key points.

Before and After also allows for the expression of views and opinions on a particular subject to come out (from the *before* questions) enabling the trainer to appreciate some of the attitudes that may exist within the group.

PURPOSE AND PRINCIPLES

The Before and After method has similarities to Info Hunt, except that, with Before and After, people do not have the written material to work through from the start, nor do they refer to the material when answering the *after* questions.

This means that there is a pre- and post-testing element to the activity that allows you to identify, and quantify if necessary, how much knowledge has been gained. If their pre- and post-reading scores are made known to them, the process also allows people to quantify for themselves how much they have learned.

The method can also allow you to identify the level of knowledge that is already held on the subject matter (which can be useful in judging how to pitch the rest of the session).

Before and After can be run as a small-group or individual activity. Small-group activities often work best, as there can be some discussion and debate about the answers. There is also less pressure when individual performance is not being judged.

PREPARATION

As with the other active-reading methods, Before and After questions or statements must refer to important items of information to be learned.

The simplest way to prepare for this activity is to devise a set of true/false statements with columns to be ticked under the headings of *Before Reading* and *After Reading*, as shown in Figure A6.1, which also shows the kind of instructions you could give to people on how to carry out the activity.

You could also use short-answer and/or multiple-choice questions as described in the Info Hunt chapter if you wanted a wider variety of question types. The example below shows the instructions on how to carry out the activity at the top of the page. These could be printed onto a separate sheet if you wish.

BEFORE & AFTER QUESTIONS

You will shortly be given some material to read about diabetes. Before reading this, please put a tick next to each statement that you think is **true** in the 'BEFORE READING' column. Then, put this sheet to one side and read the material you will be given. When you have read the material, place a tick in the AFTER READING column next to each statement that you now think is true. Please be prepared to discuss your responses after each stage.

BEFORE READING (True)	DIABETES AWARENESS	AFTER READING (True)
	The internal organ that naturally produces insulin is the pancreas	
	The term 'diabetes mellitus' is Greek in origin, and means 'the passing through of honey'	
	Hypoglycaemia occurs when blood glucose levels are higher than normal	
	Insulin can be taken in tablet form	
	Type 1 diabetes is also know as 'insulin dependent diabetes mellitus' (IDDM)	
	The occurrence of diabetes is spread almost equally across all racial and ethnic groups	
	It is possible for Type 2 diabetes to be treated by diet alone	
	In the UK there are approximately one million people with undiagnosed Type 2 diabetes	

Figure A6.1   Before and After question sheet 1

The Before and After method works very well with technical or factual information that people will not know very much about beforehand. This reduces the amount of guesswork or 'common sense' that can be applied, as in the diabetes awareness example in Figure A6.1.

The method can also be used for 'softer' types of information, however, as in Figure A6.2. In this example, the questions are not required to be responded to on a 'true/false' basis. The questions do not relate simply to facts, they are more hypothetical, and are used instead to enable participants to think about possible options. The written material that would follow would confirm if the options were viable, and possibly inform about other options not yet considered.

BEFORE & AFTER QUESTIONS

You will shortly be given some material to read about the organization's new code of practice. Before reading this, please note some brief answers to the questions posed on the left hand side in the 'BEFORE READING' column.

On completion, put this sheet to one side and read the material you will be given. When you have read the material, please adjust any of your answers in the 'AFTER READING' if appropriate.

Please be prepared to discuss your responses after each stage.

QUESTION	'BEFORE' ANSWER	'AFTER' ANSWER (if different)
What should you do if you are asked to act in a way that is inconsistent with the code?		
What should you do if you become aware that a colleague or a member of your staff has acted in breach of the code?		
What should you expect to happen if you do not comply with the code?		
What can you do if you think that a decision relating to a breach of the code is unfair?		
What should you do if you do not get a reasonable response to any concerns that you raise about the code?		

Figure A6.2   Before and After question sheet 2

RUNNING THE ACTIVITY

Briefing

The way that the activity works will need to be explained clearly. If you use Before and After sheets similar to the examples given, the instructions are already provided, so you will only need to reiterate the essential points of these or otherwise just check the participants' understanding. Also let the participants know how much time they have for each stage.

BEFORE & AFTER QUESTIONS — DIABETES AWARENESS

BEFORE READING (True)	DIABETES AWARENESS	AFTER READING (True)
X	The internal organ that naturally produces insulin is the pancreas	✓
X	The term Diabetes Mellitus is Greek in origin, and means "The passing through of honey"	✓
X	Hypoglycaemia occurs when blood glucose levels are higher than normal	✓
X	Insulin can be taken in tablet form	✓
X	Type 1 diabetes is also know as 'insulin dependent diabetes mellitus' (IDDM).	✓
X	The occurrence of diabetes is spread almost equally across all racial and ethnic groups	✓
X	It is possible for Type 2 diabetes to be treated by diet alone	✓
X	In the UK there are approximately one million people with undiagnosed Type 2 diabetes	✓

You may prefer to just produce and issue the question sheets and then brief the group orally, without any specific written instructions.

One important element of the briefing is to let the participants know that it is not important if they do not get any questions right in the *before* round. In fact, it would show a greater degree of learning if any participant had a zero *before* score, followed by a maximum *after* score.

Monitoring

The only monitoring you will probably need to do for this activity is to keep an eye on the time and how the participants are progressing. This activity is not meant to be a formal test so you have the discretion to allow a little more time for the completion of any of the stages if necessary.

Reviewing

When people have answered the *before* questions, review their responses without telling them whether or not they are correct. This will give you a feel for their current level of knowledge.

If they get all the answers right, still continue with the activity. Allowing them to read the material and see their answers confirmed in black and white may provide a worthwhile sense of achievement. (Although beware that if the questions are too easy, some people may feel patronized.)

Review the *after* results and check on the differences in people's answers. Ensure that any answers that are still incorrect or disputed are dealt with in a way that provides the rationale for what is considered to be the correct answer.

You can also review the activity as a whole by asking questions such as the following (especially for the 'softer' kind of information):

- Any surprises?
- Any disagreements – if so, why?
- Any general or other conclusions to be drawn?
- What can you apply in the future?

Do not worry if you get the response that many of the answers were just a matter of 'common sense' and thus pretty obvious. It is likely that the information only became obvious to the participants after they saw it in the form of the written statements or questions; if people had been simply asked to write down what they thought were the key elements of the topic, many of the points would have been omitted.

EXAMPLES OF USE

This activity has been used on a number of courses and sessions including one session on ethics and another on the subject of feedback. The ethics session involved asking participants some *before* questions on ethical issues along the lines of the questions shown in Figure A6.2 above. These questions were worked on in pairs, and, when they had answered them, the participants were handed out copies of relevant parts of a new code of conduct that was being introduced within their organization. They then answered the *after* questions having read the code. The activity highlighted the elements of the code that were new, and some elements that were not new, but not known to all.

The feedback Before and After activity involved a series of *before* questions which were made up of examples of a mixture of good and bad feedback being given by one person to another. On completion, in pairs, a handout was issued that provided guidelines on giving effective feedback. After reading this, the answers were revisited and any differences explored. This activity highlighted how some new managers could have some rather 'old-fashioned' ideas about what constituted effective feedback! These views may not have come out until much later in the course (if at all) without this opportunity to capture some of their views and attitudes through the *before* series of questions.

SUMMARY

HOW IT WORKS	**Trainer** • Issue individuals or groups with written questions about the relevant subject matter, to be answered before reading about it • Issue the written material about the subject • Ask the participants to answer the same questions after they have read the material – without referring to it **Groups** • Answer the before questions, read the material, then answer the after questions as above **Trainer** • Review the results and pay particular attention to differences in the Before and After scores
WHY IT WORKS	• Enables reading to be focused and concentrated • In tune with people's desire to see if their before answers were correct • Can allow trainer to identify existing attitudes or views on certain subjects
PURPOSE AND PRINCIPLES	• Similar principles to Info Hunt, but more of a test (especially if used as an activity for individuals to complete) • Provides an indicator of the starting level of knowledge of the subject • Provides an indicator of the increase in knowledge through the reading
PREPARATION	**Find suitable material** • Can use factual material from which you can easily extrapolate a number of true/false, or other question types • Can also use 'softer' material with hypothetical questions to promote the consideration of different options
RUNNING	**Briefing** • Provide written or verbal instructions about the process • Inform of the amount of time available for each stage • Inform that it is not important if before scores are low **Monitoring** • Check on timings and how the groups or individuals are progressing • Use your discretion to allow a little more time if necessary **Reviewing** • Review the before answers without divulging whether or not they are correct (continue even if they are all correct) • Review the after answers and discuss any differences • Ask questions to review the learning or conclusions to be drawn • Ensure that all participants are aware of the correct answers and the reasoning behind them before moving on

Part 3
Card-Sort Activities

Category Cards

HOW IT WORKS

1   You issue a set of cards to each group undertaking the activity. The cards sets are made up of:

   •   heading cards
   •   information cards that fit under each of the heading cards (in random order).

2   You ask the groups to stick up the heading cards, and then place the information cards under the correct heading (that is, under the correct category).

3   You review the accuracy of each group's information card placement.

4   You issue a handout to show the correct information.

WHY IT WORKS

Category Cards works within the Accelerated Learning principles of appealing to a range of different senses. With this activity, and the other card-sort activities described in the following chapters, learning is enhanced by the use of colour, shape, movement, touch and the sounds of people talking.

This method also promotes discussion and debate about the subject matter, and as mentioned at the beginning of the book, it is a prime example of 'Giving people the answers to find their meaning' rather than 'Asking them questions to find the answers'.

PURPOSE AND PRINCIPLES

The purpose of Category Cards is to provide people with the kind of information that might otherwise be delivered in a more traditional presentation or 'input' style. This method can do the job more quickly and generally more effectively.

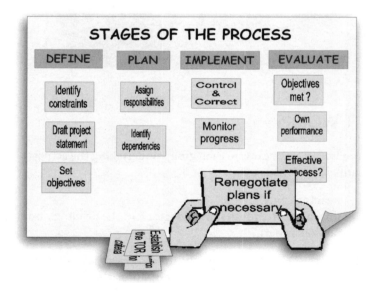

Participants have to read and consider each card to determine which heading it should be placed under. Category Cards also therefore encourages people to think things through for themselves, whilst also hearing and acting upon the thoughts and ideas of others.

PREPARATION

Category Cards is effective where you have information to give that fits securely under particular categories or headings.

The scope for the use of this type of card-sort activity is wide. Table A7.1 shows just a few of the types of content for which you can use Category Cards.

Table A7.1 Use of Category Cards

HEADING CARDS	POSSIBLE CONTENT OF INFORMATION CARDS
The elements of a model or theory (Maslow and the hierarchy of needs, for example)	The key aspects of each element Relevant actions to take regarding each element
The stages of a task or process	What has to be done at each stage? Who is responsible for each stage?
Different divisions within the organization	What each division does or is responsible for The staffing of each division and individual responsibilities
Organizational policies	The scope and content of each policy area Mini case studies for each policy area Actions to be taken for each policy area
Organizational values	What each of the values entails What should be done/not done to comply with the values
Different methods, techniques or ways of doing things	How/when to apply them Advantages/disadvantages of each When/when not to use them

If possible aim to have four or five information cards to be placed under each of two to five heading cards. Too much more than this might be too daunting a task for the participants.

If you are getting groups to stick their cards onto flipchart paper, you could have the headings already written onto the sheets and only issue the information cards. After you have made your cards, make sure that they will fit within the boundaries of your flipchart sheets. Test them out.

When reviewing Category Cards activities it can sometimes be difficult for the facilitator to remember the headings under which each card should correctly be placed. To solve this problem you can use a code system to help you (and eventually the participants) determine if they have placed the cards under the correct heading. You type the code in small text in one of the corners of each information card.

For example, let's say that your heading cards relate to a four-stage process, you could type numbers in the bottom corner of each information card as in the example in Figure A7.1.

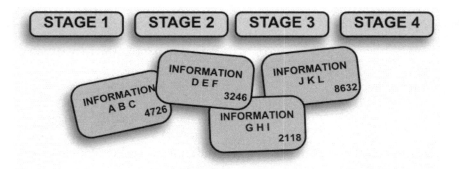

Figure A7.1   Category Cards – code

In this code, the *third* number in the series indicates the number of the correct heading card for that particular information card. (So the information card with 4726 written on it would fit under the Stage 2 heading card; information card 3246 would fit under the Stage 4 heading card; and so on).

You could also easily produce a coding system like this with letters or words, with for example, the *second* letter of a word relating to the first letter of the first word on the heading card.

(Of course you only tell the participants about the code after they have completed the activity!)

It is also possible to ask groups to produce a more complex flipchart sheet if you prepare a template beforehand. An example is shown below. If you wish, you could have the cards colour-coded to make completion a little easier.

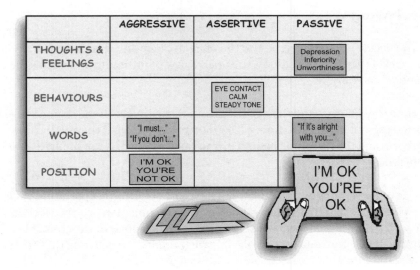

	AGGRESSIVE	ASSERTIVE	PASSIVE
THOUGHTS & FEELINGS			Depression Inferiority Unworthiness
BEHAVIOURS		EYE CONTACT CALM STEADY TONE	
WORDS	"I must..." "If you don't..."		"If it's alright with you..."
POSITION	I'M OK YOU'RE NOT OK		

I'M OK YOU'RE OK

As part of the preparation, you will also need to prepare a set of handouts to issue at the end of the activity. If possible, try to show all the information in the same way that you expect the cards to look like once they have all been placed correctly. In effect it should look like a miniature version of the completed flipchart sheet (on A4 paper rather than A1).

RUNNING THE ACTIVITY

Briefing

Introduce the topic, issue the cards to the groups and explain what they have to do. Ensure that everyone is clear about the purpose and process of the activity. Make sure that all the groups have the cards they need, the flipchart paper and any substance needed for sticking the cards to the flipchart (Blu-tac or adhesive spray, for example).

Monitoring

You must decide the extent to which you monitor each group. If you do decide to monitor, you will then need to decide if you are going to intervene if they make mistakes.

If you decide to intervene when they are going off track, do so by asking questions of their rationale and thought processes, rather than just pointing out what's wrong. If you are using a code, try not to give this away.

If you are monitoring two or three groups, aim to give them approximately equal amounts of your time, unless any particular group is really struggling.

Reviewing

If you decide not to intervene and therefore not help any groups to get back on track if they are going astray, the final review of the results will need to be handled carefully.

A good way of reviewing this type of exercise is to display all the results and ask for a representative or two from each group to explain what they have come up with, and the reasoning behind it. You can then discuss the similarities and differences.

If one or two groups or individuals have got cards in incorrect positions, there is a possibility that they might get defensive or argumentative if they feel that they are losing face in front of others. This approach does, however, enable the often valuable learning process of comparing results and debating the different issues and thought processes.

By the end of the activity everyone must be aware of the correct answers or card placements, and issuing the handout can reinforce this.

Explaining the code and dealing with any questions will also be required at some point near the end of the activity. Depending on the nature of the subject matter, you may need to lead further discussions or explore the implications of what has been learned, and possibly its application in the work environment.

EXAMPLES OF USE

Category Cards have been used on various courses for various topics. Some examples include:

Learning styles

Four heading cards were issued, with information cards relating to different types of learning activity. Groups were then asked to match the learning activities to each style. This activity promoted quite a lot of debate. Many cards were placed under one heading only to be discussed further and then moved (usually to the correct heading).

The review included asking people how much they agreed with the activities associated with their own preferred style.

Assertiveness

A more complex table was created to show the thoughts, feelings and so on associated with assertion, aggression and passivity. Though more complex, this was not difficult to complete. Groups were generally able to finish it correctly within ten minutes. (I even thought at times that I should try to make it more stretching!)

Ethics training

Groups were given heading cards showing the four (new) key ethical values of their organiaation. The information cards showed bullet points of actions that the participants (as managers) must do and must not do in terms of the four values. These had to be matched to the correct ethical value.

SUMMARY

HOW IT WORKS	**Trainer** • Issue a set of cards to each group: – heading cards and information cards **Groups** • Stick up the heading cards, and then stick up the information cards under the correct heading **Trainer** • Review results • Issue full handout showing correct headings and information
WHY IT WORKS	• Appeals to a range of different senses • Includes colour, shape, movement, discussion • Example of 'giving people the answers to find their meaning'
PURPOSE AND PRINCIPLES	• Provision of knowledge that might otherwise be delivered in a presentational style, or through a participative question/answer approach • Groups still required to think through and discuss information, but in a more focused way
PREPARATION	**Find suitable source material** • Existing information that fits securely under particular categories or headings • Aim for material that can have four or five information cards under each of two to five headings **Produce the cards and other materials** • Make sure size of cards allows them all to be placed within the space available, a flipchart sheet for example. • Consider using a code to make it easy to identify if the card is in the right place at the end of the activity • Draw up in advance a flipchart sheet if necessary as a template for a more complex display if necessary • Prepare and print handouts in a similar style to a completed card display
RUNNING	**Briefing** • Explain purpose of activity and provide written or verbal instructions • Issue all cards, flipchart sheets and adhesive materials as needed **Monitoring** • Can intervene to assist if necessary, but avoid giving away the code if using one • Usually preferable to wait before intervening as groups may identify errors for themselves as discussions progress **Reviewing** • May need to be handled carefully if you allow groups to come back with incorrect placements – but can have greater learning impact • Ask for representatives from each group to talk through their results discus similarities and differences • Ask questions to check rationale behind any incorrect placements • Explain the code if used, and ensure everybody is clear on correct placements by the end

NDE Cards

HOW IT WORKS

1 You issue a set of cards (possibly colour coded) to small groups and ask them to arrange the cards into the sequence of name/definition/example (NDE).
2 You observe their progress and help out if necessary.
3 You review the accuracy of the groups' results and discuss any issues or questions arising.
4 You issue a handout of the correct information.

WHY IT WORKS

As in all of the card-sort activities, during the NDE Cards activity people need to read the cards, discuss their content, take in their meaning, consider where they should go and physically place them in the appropriate position.

Also like the other card-sort activities the NDE Card approach involves colour, movement and the tactile handling of the cards.

NDE cards work because they provide definitions of particular types of things (names). The cards then provide specific examples to be associated with the name and definitions. The examples help to reinforce the meaning of the names. They also put them into context, give them relevance, and bring them to life.

Once again, because participants are given the answers, they do not have to think them through in the same way as if they were asked to produce definitions and examples for themselves. Having to do so often confuses people and allows them to drift (or send others) down the wrong track. They have to think about what they have in front of them, and make sense and order out of what is written on the cards.

PURPOSE AND PRINCIPLES

The NDE Cards activity enables participants to gain knowledge relating to a subject matter which needs to be defined before it can be understood. It is an activity that often works well as a precursor to a skills-practice exercise or case study.

It is a little like a jigsaw puzzle with words. It is similar to the Category Cards activity (Activity 7) and, once again, it is a method that can be used as a substitute for delivering a straight 'input' presentation on the subject.

This is the method that was described earlier in the book when it was used to replace a long question-and-answer session on some of the various types of questions that trainers can use.

PREPARATION

NDE cards are best used when you can easily identify information that is naturally split into certain 'types' such as the 'types of question' example given above. You need to have things with definite and accepted names.

You can apply a colour-coding system to differentiate between the name, definition and example cards (see Figure A8.1). This will make the completion of the activity a little easier (and more colourful).

A coding system can also be used to help the participants, and possibly yourself, to identify whether or not the cards have been placed in the correct position. Your system can be similar to the one used for the Category Cards activity, but adjusted to take account of the fact that you need to match the name cards with their relevant definition and example cards.

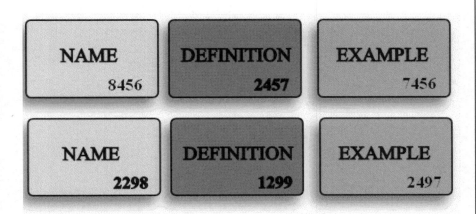

Figure A8.1   NDE Cards – code

In the example shown, the *third* number in the sequence determines the cards that match. So the cards above are all in their correct NDE positions (three fives and three nines).

If you use a coding system like this for NDE Cards and also use other card-sort methods with codes on the same training event, there is a danger that people will start to try and work out the code instead of working on the contents of the cards. You can reduce the likelihood of this by making the code almost impossible to break, so that people will not even try. You can do this by either making the numeric code longer (five or six numbers) and also by repeating the code numbers in other parts of the sequence. For example, code number 1299 above. This should allow participants to give most concentration to placing the cards correctly from the information they contain, rather than from breaking the code.

Of course, you could omit the codes altogether, but this might deprive you of a tool for enabling groups to move the cards into the correct positions themselves before they are explained. It would also make the reviewing process longer if you were to check through all the cards individually to see if they were in the right place.

Depending on the quantity of cards, you may need to check that they will all fit in the space available (flipchart/wall/whiteboard/floor) beforehand.

You will need to produce a handout of the correct information and, as in the Category Cards activity, this should match the layout of the correctly positioned NDE cards as much as possible. Producing the handout in a table form should make it similar enough.

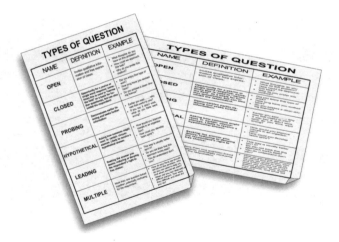

RUNNING THE ACTIVITY

Briefing

This activity can be run in the same way as the Category Cards activity, where groups are issued with the cards and flipchart sheets and asked to stick them in the appropriate places. The same kind of briefing about the purpose of the activity and the logistical arrangements will also need to given.

Monitoring

You will need to consider the extent to which you intervene as the groups are placing the cards, especially if they are placing cards in incorrect positions. Again, the same considerations apply here as with Category Cards.

Reviewing

The usual way of reviewing this activity is to allow the groups to view each other's work and identify any differences, which can then be discussed and clarified by you if necessary.

An optional approach to check the groups' understanding of the names and definitions is to ask *them* to write the examples on blank pieces of card that they can then put up in the correct position. This can add to the time, however, and you may have the old problem of dealing with incorrect examples.

Examples of use

As already mentioned the NDE Cards method has been used as part of a wider session on 'Types of Question' and their use in training. That example also included the use of Traffic Lights (Activity 9).

NDE cards have also been used in training on assertiveness. For this event the names were the names of different types of assertive behaviour. These then had their respective definition cards, and then cards with examples of the words that could be used when applying each type of assertive behaviour.

You will see another dimension to NDE cards in the Washing Line (Activity 12).

SUMMARY

HOW IT WORKS	**Trainer**
	• Issue a set of cards to each group:
	  – Heading cards of NAME/DEFINITION/EXAMPLE
	  – Cards with Names/Definitions/Examples of the subject matter
	Groups
	• Stick up the NDE heading cards, and then stick up the Information cards under the correct heading
	Trainer
	• Review results
	• Issue full handout showing correct names, definitions and examples

WHY IT WORKS	• Appeals to a range of different senses • Includes colour, shape, movement, discussion • Example of 'giving people the answers to find their meaning' • Definitions reinforce meaning of the names. Examples put them into context and bring them to life
PURPOSE AND PRINCIPLES	• Provision of knowledge in similar way to Category Cards • Groups still required to think through and discuss information, but in a more focused way • Can be used a precursor to a skills-practice or case-study exercise
PREPARATION	**Find suitable source material** • Existing information on topics that can be split into particular 'types' with definite names • Consider producing all name cards in one colour, all definition cards in another colour and example cards in a third colour to make things less complicated **Produce the cards and other materials** • Make sure size of cards allows them all to be placed within the space available, a flipchart sheet for example • Consider using a coding system to make it easy to identify if the card is in the right place at the end of the activity • Prepare and print handouts in a similar style to a completed card display
RUNNING	**Briefing** • Explain purpose of activity and provide written or verbal instructions • Issue all cards, flipchart sheets and adhesive materials as needed **Monitoring** • Similar monitoring options as for Category Cards – intervene if necessary, but may be better not to **Reviewing** • May need to be handled carefully if you allow groups to come back with incorrect placements – but can have greater learning impact • Ask for representatives from each group to talk through their results discus similarities and differences • Ask questions to check rationale behind any incorrect placements • Explain the code if used, and ensure everybody is clear on correct placements by the end

Traffic Lights

HOW IT WORKS

1   You issue a set of cards to each of two or more small groups, and explain
    the purpose and process of the activity. Each set of cards contain
    statements or pieces of information that can be considered under
    categories such as:

    •   good, bad or indifferent;
    •   true, false or debatable;
    •   correct, incorrect or uncertain;
    •   yes, no or maybe;
    •   always, never or sometimes.

The set of cards also includes three circular 'traffic light' cards coloured
green, amber and red.

2   You ask the groups to place the main set of cards under what they
     believe is the appropriate traffic light, as in the Category Cards activity
     (Activity 7).
3   You review and compare the groups' results, discussing the rationale
     behind their responses and issuing any handouts to show the correct
     answers.

WHY IT WORKS

The Traffic Light activity is a good method for encouraging debate and
identifying areas where views and opinions can conflict. It can be a highly
effective method to dispel common misconceptions about various topics. It can
also be an effective way of identifying 'grey areas' where there is no absolute
right or wrong answer (see Figure A9.1).

The amber traffic light can be especially useful in that it can be used as a means
of 'parking' any areas of disagreement for discussion and clarification at a later
stage. It also gives tacit acknowledgement that it is OK to have doubts and
uncertainties about some things, and that 'we don't know' is an acceptable
response and a good starting point for learning.

Figure A9.1   Traffic lights – possible meanings

PURPOSE AND PRINCIPLES

The principle behind Traffic Lights is that sometimes there are definite
divisions of things into good and bad, right and wrong etc. (green and red) but
sometimes the divisions are not so clear cut (red *amber* green).

Times and fashions change. The example shows questions that might be
asked of a job applicant at a competence-based interview. Some are 'good'

competency/behavioural questions, others are 'bad', and some *can* be used – but with certain provisos.

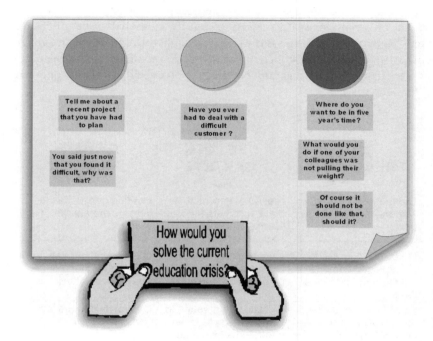

In this example, many of the 'bad' questions would have been considered acceptable in the past; before the competence/behavioural approach became prominent. Anyone who had been subjected to the older style of questioning would therefore be able to identify how things had changed. This is a principle that could apply to many areas as times and processes change or evolve.

PREPARATION

The subject matter to choose for Traffic Lights can vary greatly, but whatever the topic, you will need to be sure that the information cards can be placed under one of the lights.

When preparing the information cards, be sure that what is written on them will follow grammatically or conceptually from what you want the traffic lights to represent. So if you want the lights to represent true/false/uncertain, then you must have *statements* written on the cards that could be either true or false. Similarly, if you are using the lights as good and bad, you will need the cards to show *examples* that could be either good or bad.

It might be preferable on occasion to prepare written instructions to be issued to the groups as something they can refer to during the activity to help keep them on track.

You may only want to use the exercise to identify issues that are definitely green or red – right or wrong. If this is the case, you could use just the red and green lights, without including amber. Alternatively, you could use the amber light as a place to put cards that cannot be agreed upon as being either red or green – the 'parking space'.

USE FREQUENTLY	USE WITH CAUTION	DO NOT USE
Open questions that enable the interviewee to talk	Closed questions that do not promote the interviewee to talk freely	Leading questions that indicate the answer you want
Questions that ask for examples of demonstrating the required behaviours	Questions relating to the individuals general competence in a particular area	Questions that relate to areas other than competences and behaviours
Questions that probe into the individual's reasoning behind their actions	Questions that relate to competences held/demonstrated a long time ago	Questions that are long and convoluted
Questions that probe into the outcomes and results of the individual's actions	Questions with implications relating to employment law and equal opportunities legislation	Questions that make the interviewee think "What do they want to hear?"

Handouts are also likely to be required to be issued at the end. You can use the actual traffic light layout for the handouts, showing what should be placed where, with an indicator of what each traffic light actually means (yes/no/maybe, always/seldom/never, and so on). This will be fine if you have a colour printer. If not, a handout in table form with just the definitions of the traffic lights at the top will suffice.

RUNNING THE ACTIVITY

Briefing

You will need to explain the process of the activity and the meanings of the traffic lights clearly, perhaps using written instructions. Depending on the nature of the topic and the use of the traffic lights, you may want to reassure people that there is nothing wrong with not knowing everything, and that it will be totally acceptable to place some items under the amber ('don't know') traffic light.

Monitoring

As in most of the other card-sort activities you can monitor groups' progress during Traffic Lights in a 'hands-on' or 'hands-off' way depending on how you intend to review it.

In most cases it will probably be appropriate to maintain a 'hands-off' approach and not intervene to put people back on track if they are straying from it. Usually, the differences between the groups' results will lead to the most productive learning. However, some intervention may be necessary if a group is going way off track or otherwise struggling.

Reviewing

Like many of the card-sort activities, Traffic Lights can be reviewed by asking a spokesperson from each group to explain their results and the thinking behind them. Any differences between the groups' results can then be explored and clarified where necessary.

If you want all cards to be placed under red and green only by the end of the activity, with the amber light as just 'parking space', the review will need to concentrate some time on the cards under the amber light to explain where each of the cards should actually be. If you achieve agreement and understanding of the correct placements of any amber cards, you will get a good indication of the amount of new learning that has taken place.

If the Traffic Lights method is used to explore areas that can be subject to valid differences of opinion, the review of the exercise could also focus on the behaviours of individuals during the completion of the activity – such as:

- offering suggestions and opinions;
- supporting the views of others;
- challenging the views of others (assertively or aggressively);
- leading the proceedings;
- dominating the proceedings;
- keeping proceedings on track;
- withdrawing from the proceedings.

More information on running activities like this as a 'communication exercise' can be found in the Highlight Hierarchy chapter (Activity 5).

EXAMPLES OF USE

As mentioned earlier in this chapter, Traffic Lights have been used in the area of recruitment interviewing where there can be a number of misconceptions as to what constitutes good or bad interview questions, and some controversy!

If you are using Traffic Lights in an area like this where some understandable misconceptions may exist from personal experience, you will need to be sure what really is good and bad as far as your (or your client's) organization is concerned. For example, a job interview question along the lines of 'What would you say is the colour of ambition?' would be placed under a red traffic light in most organizations I have worked for, but it might be placed under a green light in others.

At the beginning of the book, the example was also described of using Traffic Lights as an add-on element to a (NDE) card-sort activity relating to types of questions to use as a trainer, where there were some definite red cards (multiple questions, leading questions) some definite green cards (open questions, probing questions) and some 'use with caution' amber cards (closed questions, hypothetical questions) which were appropriate to use with provisos.

SUMMARY

HOW IT WORKS	**Trainer**
	• Issue a set of cards to each group:
	   – Green, amber, red circular cards (Traffic Lights)
	   – Cards with statements that can fit within categories such as good/bad/indifferent yes/no/maybe
	Groups
	• Stick up the statements under what they believe to be the correct traffic light
	Trainer
	• Review results and discuss issues
	• Issue full handout showing correct or generally accepted answers

WHY IT WORKS	• Encourages debate and identifying areas where views can conflict and where there is no absolute right or wrong answer • Allows for 'parking' of issues for later discussion • Gives tacit acknowledgement that it is OK not to know everything!
PURPOSE AND PRINCIPLES	• Used to identify definite good/bad right/wrong issues, and also issues that are not so clear cut • Used also to highlight areas where accepted, and acceptable, ways of doing things may have changed • Can be used as activity for demonstration of communication and interpersonal skills, with less importance placed on the content of the exercise
PREPARATION	**Find suitable source material** • Ensure that the statement cards can be placed under one of the traffic lights • Can use material that only requires red/green traffic lights **Produce the cards and other materials** • Ensure that the statement cards follow grammatically and conceptually from what each traffic light colour represents • Draft and print instructions and traffic light definitions for reference during the activity if required • Prepare and print handouts in a similar style to a completed card display
RUNNING	**Briefing** • Explain purpose of activity and provide written or verbal instructions • Ensure meaning of each traffic light is understood • Reassure participants about amber 'don't know' responses being acceptable • Issue all cards, flipchart sheets and adhesive materials as needed **Monitoring** • Similar monitoring options as for category cards – intervene if necessary, but may be better not to **Reviewing** • Ask for representatives from each group to talk through their results discus similarities and differences • Spend proportionately more time on the amber cards if necessary • Review communication skills if activity used for this purpose

Now What's the Question?

HOW IT WORKS

1   You issue two sets of cards to one or more teams.

   •   One set has a question on every card (on perhaps yellow-coloured card).
   •   The other set of is made up of answers to those questions (on perhaps orange-coloured card).

2   You ask the teams to match the answers to the questions and display them on a flipchart or whiteboard.

3   On completion, you ask the teams to present their findings and discuss any issues arising.

4   You issue handouts to show the questions and answers.

WHY IT WORKS

As described in the introduction to this book, trainers often ask questions of groups verbally to help them learn by working out the answers for themselves. Problems can sometimes arise with this approach, however:

- People may answer incorrectly – and some trainers find it difficult to deal with incorrect answers without appearing to put the person down.
- People may just take stabs and guess at the answer without thinking.
- People may just give the answers that they think you want to hear.
- Sometimes the questions may be too difficult to answer.
- Sometimes you just get a stony or uncomfortable silence.
- People may get hold of the wrong end of the stick, or answer from an unexpected viewpoint.
- Phrasing a question that is easily understood and elicits a particular desired answer, is not easy.
- Discussions stemming from the question or answer can easily go off on a tangent.
- One or more people monopolizes the group and answers all the questions.

Now, What's the Question? does a lot to minimize or alleviate these potential problems.

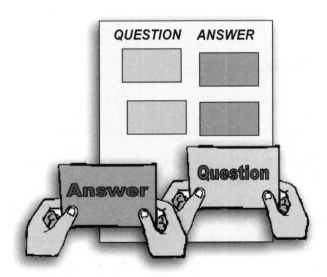

PURPOSE AND PRINCIPLES

Now, What's the Question? is an effective method to use when the answers to the questions that you provide are not too obvious, but can be considered, discussed and worked out by the teams. It is used when there is particular factual information to be learned, which does not involve the exploration of views or opinions, but will be either right or wrong.

You could use this activity on a wide range of subjects. It will work with theoretical, background and technical knowledge. The example cards shown in Figure A10.1 relate to Maslow's hierarchy of needs theory and Herzberg's theory of motivators and hygiene factors.

Figure A10.1 Examples of question and answer cards

Used in this way, the activity could be used as an introduction to the topic, with further details and concepts explored afterwards.

You could also of course use Now, What's the Question? as an evaluation method to test knowledge and understanding at the end of a session.

In fact you could use it at the beginning *and* at the end of a session. The results of the initial exercise could be left on display without review or amendment, and at the end of the session the teams are asked to look at their results and make adjustments if they need to.

PREPARATION

From the material that you usually use for a particular session, you should quite easily be able to extrapolate some facts of pieces of information to use as 'answers'. Then it is a matter of drafting a question to match each answer. When you draft the question, make sure that it matches the answer grammatically as well as in its content.

About six to ten question-and-answer cards should be sufficient for groups to spend a reasonable amount of time on the activity.

When you have drafted the questions and answers, test them out to make sure that the questions do match the answers, and that they are neither too difficult nor too easy to match. Testing out will also allow you to check the timings, and ensure that all the cards will fit on a sheet of flipchart paper, if that is where they are going to be eventually displayed.

As an option, you could prepare more answer cards than question cards – with the extra cards showing incorrect answers as red herrings. The teams then have the added task of determining the correct from the incorrect.

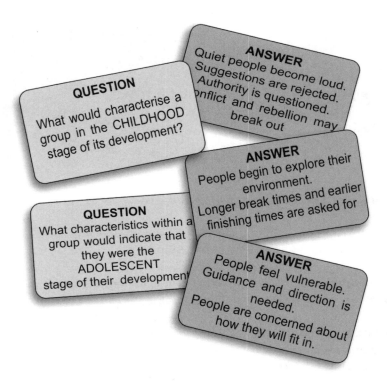

Similar to the Category Cards and NDE Cards activities, you could develop a coding system to enable correctly or incorrectly matched cards to be identified easily.

A handout of all the questions and answers will also be needed. This should be produced in a similar format to the way you would like to see the cards displayed by the participants. A simple table to show the questions down one column and the respective answers opposite in another column should work fine.

RUNNING THE ACTIVITY

Briefing

As usual, inform the groups about the purpose of the activity, the logistical arrangements and the timings. Inform them too if a spokesperson will be required to explain each group's results on completion.

Like most of the card-sort activities, this one is probably best conducted in small groups, either within the main room or in syndicate rooms. If syndicates are used, the groups should usually come back into the main room for the review with their cards stuck appropriately onto flipchart paper.

Monitoring

It will be worthwhile to wander around the room (or rooms) to check on the progress of all the groups. As with some of the other card-sort and active-reading activities, beware of intervening too quickly. This is another activity where a group can place a card in an incorrect place that is likely to be identified as an error later when other cards do not seem to fit anywhere, and they will be forced to reconsider.

You again have the choice of intervening to get groups onto the right track if they are straying or leaving them alone until the review.

Reviewing

When reviewing this activity, the usual approach is to ask each group in turn to state one question and its answer. You then ask if the other groups agree or not, discuss as necessary and then move on to another group and another question and answer.

If the groups have placed their cards onto flipchart, they should all match horizontally, showing the correct question and answer. They are unlikely to match vertically, however. The groups will put their cards in different orders down the flipchart sheet. If all the groups' flipcharts are displayed in the room together, it will be your job to tick off or otherwise indicate which questions and answers have been covered in the review.

An alternative approach to prevent any confusion about which question and answer cards have been reviewed would be to number the question cards, and ask the groups to display them in that order down the flipchart sheet.

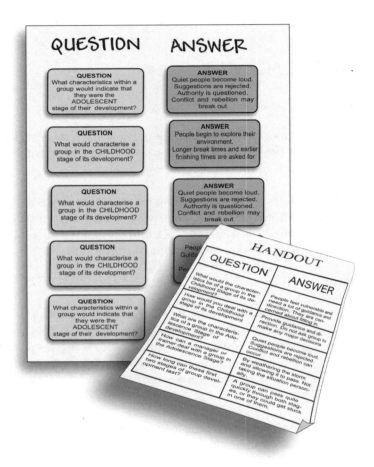

You could also just issue the handout, and ask the groups to identify if there are any differences for themselves.

EXAMPLE OF USE

This activity has been used for the subject of motivation, as per some of the example cards shown in this chapter. There was a slight variation in that two different groups were asked to match the questions and answers to two different motivation theories (Herzberg's and Maslow's).

Monitoring the activity with this approach involved some trainer intervention in order to ensure that each group had the correct matches before the review. This was because the review consisted of each group presenting their findings to the other, and explaining the rationale behind each of their answer cards. On this occasion, therefore, it was important that the groups had the correct matches before their presentation, to ensure that the other group received only the correct information.

NOT JUST QUESTIONS AND ANSWERS

Depending on the material you have, or what you want people to learn, you could also use the 'matching' principle of Now, What's the Question? in order to match things like:

- problems and solutions
- causes and effects
- people/work areas and their responsibilities
- actions and consequences.

And there are probably others that you can think of too.

SUMMARY

HOW IT WORKS	**Trainer**
	 • Issue two sets of cards to each group:
	   – One set with questions written on them (on say yellow-coloured card)
	   – One set with the answers written on them (on say orange-coloured card)
	 Groups
	 • Asked to match the questions with the answers and display them, on flipchart for example
	 Trainer
	 • Review results and discuss issues
	 • Issue full handout showing correct match of questions and answers

WHY IT WORKS	• Prevents may of the problems associated with asking questions verbally • Same advantages as with other card sort exercises such as appeal to different senses, and fit with the main learning styles
PURPOSE AND PRINCIPLES	• Used to promote learning of knowledge where there are definite, but not too obvious answers to given questions • Can be useful as an introduction to a topic, before a more detailed exploration • Can also be used as an evaluation exercise, and as a pre-post evaluation to indicate the amount of knowledge gained
PREPARATION	**Find suitable source material** • A lot of material will be suitable for this method, as long as some pertinent facts and questions can be drawn from it • Use material that will enable around six to ten questions and answers to be drafted **Produce the cards and other materials** • Draft the 'answers' first – which should be the most important pieces of information to be learned • Draft the question, making sure that it matches grammatically • Consider inserting extra answer cards as red herrings if it will help prevent the exercise being too easy • Consider using a coding system similar to NDE Cards • Prepare and print handouts in a similar style to a completed card display
RUNNING	**Briefing** • Explain purpose of activity and provide written or verbal instructions • Issue all cards, flipchart sheets and adhesive materials as needed **Monitoring** • Similar monitoring options as for category cards – intervene if necessary, but may be better not to **Reviewing** • Ask for representatives from each group to talk through their results discus similarities and differences • Tick off reviewed question and answer cards as you go along

Process Cards

HOW IT WORKS

1   You issue groups with a set of cards that can be put together to make up a diagram or flowchart.
2   You ask the groups to stick up the cards in the correct sequence and with the correct connections.
3   You review the accuracy of each group's completed diagram and issue the handout of it.

WHY IT WORKS

Process Cards is a way of allowing groups to build up diagrams, but with more opportunity to develop a deeper understanding of the processes, rather than just accepting what has been presented to them. This is because they build up each element of the process until they have the full diagram, and each element can therefore be discussed by the group members themselves, or with you if necessary, and any related problems or confusion can be dealt with.

Process Cards also allow people to see the logic and purpose behind the actions required of the overall process. However, the nature of the process does not need to be always of a technical nature. The Process Cards method can be used for many types of models that are usually shown in diagrammatic form (such as the experiential learning cycle shown in Figure A11.1), which is based on the Honey Mumford model of how people can learn most effectively from their experiences.

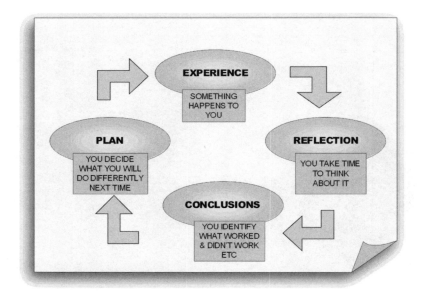

Figure A11.1 Examples of process cards (based on the Honey and Mumford learning cycle model)

PURPOSE AND PRINCIPLES

The purpose of Process Cards is to allow groups to explore sequences of actions, and identify what has to be done and when. Often, diagrams and flowcharts are shown to groups on a flipchart, or built up using PowerPoint presentations. They may also be shown in other documents, such as instruction manuals, guidance notes and so on.

Like many of the card-sort activities, Process Cards work something like the completion of a jigsaw. Unlike the other card-sort activities, however, this one can also include cards in the shapes of connecting lines or arrows, and the shapes of the cards themselves can have specific meanings.

PREPARATION

Preparation for Process Cards is simpler if you have a model or flowchart from which to work. If not, you will need to identify all the elements of the process yourself, and design the diagram or flowchart.

If you want to produce a flowchart, the most common use for the various shapes of the boxes is as shown in the diagram at Figure A11.2.

RECTANGLE OR BOX		REPRESENTS A STEP OR ACTION THAT NEEDS TO BE TAKEN WITHIN THE PROCESS. OFTEN THE MOST COMMON SYMBOL IN A FLOWCHART
ROUNDED RECTANGLE		REPRESENTS AN EVENT THAT OCCURS AUTOMATICALLY, TRIGGERING A SUBSEQUENT ACTION.
DIAMOND		REPRESENTS A DECISION POINT, USUALLY WITH 'YES' AND 'NO' BRANCHES STEMMING FROM TWO OF THE DIAMOND'S POINTS
CIRCLE		REPRESENTS A CONNECTION WITH ANOTHER PROCESS. A REFERENCE TO THE OTHER PROCESS SHOULD BE WRITTEN IN THE CIRCLE
DIRECTIONAL ARROWS		INDICATES DIRECTION OF THE FLOW OF THE PROCESS. TWO-WAY PROCESSES WILL HAVE ARROWHEADS AT BOTH ENDS
DIAMOND AND BOXES		REPRESENTS MULTIPLE CHOICES (3 OR MORE). THE CHOSEN OPTION DETERMINES THE USERS PATH THROUGH THE REST OF THE PROCESS

Figure A11.2 Process Cards – flowchart symbols

Please note that the colours of the symbols in this table are not significant. However, you could make the colours mean something specific in your diagrams if required.

All of the flowchart symbols above (and more) are available in Microsoft Word within 'AutoShapes' from the 'Drawing' toolbar. Block arrows are also available from this toolbar, which will be thicker and easier to handle than simple thin lines with arrowheads.

If you are allowing a degree of flexibility in how the final diagram might look, you can omit making arrow cards and ask the groups to draw the appropriate lines on their diagrams where *they* think they need to be.

Whether using a formal diagram or not, use a variety of colours but keep all cards of the same shape in the same colour (as with the ovals and boxes in the learning cycle model shown in Figure A11.1).

You may need to produce a 'master copy' of a completed diagram in order to help you monitor and review the groups' diagrams. You may also need copies of this as a handout to issue at the end of the activity.

RUNNING THE ACTIVITY

Briefing

As always, you will need to explain the purpose of the activity, and what is going to happen.

If you are going to use a more formal flowchart, you may need to ensure that the group is aware of what all the different shapes represent. If you are not using the formal approach, you can use any shapes that look good, although if there is a certain convention or system you are using, you may still need to tell them about it.

Monitoring

If the groups' diagrams can all look slightly different to each others, and different to your master copy, but still be correct in principle, you will need to be more careful when monitoring their progress. In this situation you will need to check out the rationale behind the build-up of their diagram to make sure that it is sound.

If there are any errors being made that are not just a matter of format, you will need to decide whether to intervene whilst monitoring, or wait until the review.

Reviewing

This will run in a similar way to other card-sort activities, with groups displaying and explaining their results, and comparing them to the other groups'. In this activity, however, there may be more differences in layout that may need to be clarified first. For example, one group may have set out their diagram in landscape format, whilst another may have used a portrait shape, or the joining arrows will lead to boxes placed in different areas of the flipchart sheet of one group to another's. It will be the content and linkages of the actual diagram that will be most important to review, so the difference in shape should be dealt with a quickly as possible. In most cases it is unlikely to matter.

A variation on the Process Cards activity that can work in some circumstances is to allow your groups to *become* the process that the diagram describes. For example, people could arrange themselves within the room holding the cards that they represent, and take on the role of one or more elements of the process. The directional arrows could be replaced by string.

The participants could then describe the process from start to finish with each person speaking at the relevant time (using their card as a prompt if required).

Example of use

This activity has been used on trainer-training courses, where participants have been given cards relating to the process of conducting training needs analysis within their particular organization. Each card showed an activity to be carried out and the participants had to develop a flowchart from the cards. (On this occasion only rectangular cards were used.)

This activity highlighted for some people that there was more to the topic than they originally thought. The flowchart diagram issued at the end was also found to be useful because it showed what needed to be done within that particular organization, and who was involved as well.

Another example of Process Cards was is one that was used on a change management training event. It was a partially completed model of the emotional processes that people go through during times of change plotted on a 'change curve' The emotions were represented by various 'smiley faces' (and some not-so-smiley).

The curve was drawn across two pieces of A3 paper, and the faces were stuck to their relevant places along the two sheets. Each sheet was then laminated and taped down the middle to join it to others and allow them to be folded. They were then sprayed with adhesive and left to go tacky.

Groups were given cards with the name of the emotion and some of the words that might be heard from people at each particular point on the curve. They were then asked to place the cards with the relevant faces at the relevant point on the curve. The finished result is shown in Figure A11.3. The complete diagram was then issued as a handout.

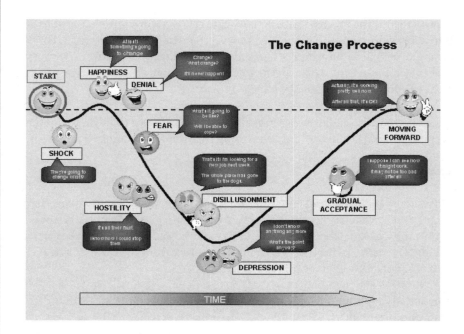

Figure A11.3 Process Cards – change curve

SUMMARY

HOW IT WORKS	**Trainer** • Issue groups with a set of cards that make up a diagram or flowchart **Groups** • Stick up the cards in the correct sequence and with correct connections if appropriate **Trainer** • Review accuracy of results and discuss issues • Issue full handout showing correct diagram or flowchart
WHY IT WORKS	• Enables deeper understanding of different elements of a process and their relationships • Each element of a diagram can be discussed and any problems or confusion dealt with • Enables people to see the logic and purpose behind a process or model
PURPOSE AND PRINCIPLES	• Used to enable groups to explore sequences of actions and identify what needs to be done when, and why. • Works like the completion of a jigsaw • For this exercise, the shapes and colours of the cards can have specific meanings
PREPARATION	**Find suitable source material** • Simpler if you already have a model, diagram or flowchart to work from • If no source material is available, you will need to draw something up using the conventional shapes if relevant **Produce the cards and other materials** • 'AutoShapes' in Microsoft Word can be used for flowchart shapes and block arrows • Arrows made of card are optional. You want the groups to draw their own • Produce a 'master copy' for monitoring purposes and as a handout • (Consider option of having the groups be the process)
RUNNING	**Briefing** • Explain purpose of activity and provide written or verbal instructions • If necessary, explain the meaning of any particular shapes or colours **Monitoring** • Be prepared for groups to put up their cards in different formats. Check for the correct connections and sequences more than the overall layout ask questions to clarify before making any direct remedial intervention **Reviewing** • Ask for representatives from each group to talk through their results discus similarities and differences • Explain that superficial differences in layout or format are not important

Washing Line

HOW IT WORKS

1   Before starting, set up one or two 'washing lines' in the room. This will usually be pieces of string tied between coat stands, or other available fixtures or fittings in the room. Their length will vary depending on the amount of 'washing' to be hung on them (see below).

2   Issue a set of T-shirts and/or other items of clothing that have pieces of information printed onto them and you ask the group(s) to hang up the items of washing on the line, in a particular order. You will also need to issue pegs or another form of clip to attach the washing to the line.

3   When the groups have hung up their washing in what they think is the correct order, you review and discuss their results and issue the relevant handouts.

WHY IT WORKS

Washing Line is another example of a card-sort activity that allows groups to consider and discuss the issues in question, whether or not there are any definite right or wrong answers. This activity can also require people to stand up and move around.

With, say, three groups hanging out their washing in the same room there can be quite a lot of buzzing, with the possibility of peeking at what the other group(s) are doing and thus provoking further discussion and comparison.

Whereas most of the other card-sort activities use standard rectangular or oval shapes, the Washing Line has the added visual and tactile elements of working with irregular but recognizable shapes (T-shirts and shorts, for example – see Figure A12.1). This tends to add even more of a 'sparkle' to the proceedings. People invariably smile when they first see the materials.

Figure A12.1 Washing Line – example T-shirts

PURPOSE AND PRINCIPLES

The purpose of the Washing Line activity is to allow people to identify actual or possible *hierarchies* or *sequences* or *levels* of things. For example, you could use it where you have a number of actions or issues that could be placed at various points on scales from:

* easy to difficult
* weak to strong
* never to always

- low to high
- unimportant to very important
- short term to long term
- start to end.

The Washing Line activity can also be used as a form of NDE (name, description, example) card-sort exercise where some sort of order or hierarchy is involved as well (see Activity 8). For example, a T-shirt might show a name and a description, and a pair of shorts might show an example that has to be placed next to (or attached to) the relevant T-shirt on the washing line.

PREPARATION

If possible try to keep the number of items of clothing between four and ten. Too many more could make the activity more complex and cumbersome for the participants.

You can put the information onto various types of washing. You could have just plain 'sheets' of paper, or you could cut out shapes of T-shirts, dresses, shorts etc, – whatever takes your fancy and is able to contain all the written information you need.

I have found that T-shirts and shorts usually work the best. I don't know exactly why, but perhaps it is because T-shirts often have text and slogans on them, they are some of the most casual items of clothing to wear, they are worn by both sexes and are reminders of warm summer days.

The easiest and simplest approach for producing them is to:

- draw and cut out the shape you want (e.g. a T-shirt) from a piece of card;
- type the words and print them onto other sheets of card (possibly card of different colours);
- place the cut-out shape over the words and draw around it with a marker pen;
- laminate the shape if possible;
- cut out the shape around the drawn outline to get your final product to be hung on the washing line.

If you have any drawing or home-publishing software for your PC you could use it to create more complex designs and without having to use a cut-out template. You could also add pictures or clip art to the items of clothing.

If you use Microsoft Word as your word processing software, experiment with WordArt and different fonts and font colours to make your information visually interesting.

You could also of course buy some iron-on transfer paper onto which you can print the T-shirt information and then transfer it onto *actual* T-shirts or other items of clothing (front and back if necessary). Small, baby or children's clothes could be used – even adult clothes if you have the room. Indeed, you could ask people to actually *wear* some T-shirts, arrange themselves in the correct order and stand along a line marked on the floor.

If possible, continue the clothing and washing-line theme into the production of any handouts; otherwise, use a table form again to show the information.

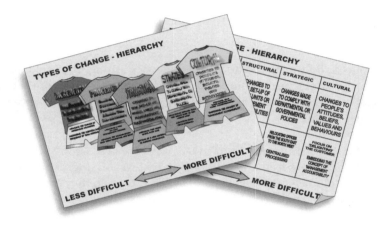

RUNNING THE ACTIVITY

Briefing

As for all activities, you will need to brief the group about the process and purpose of the activity either before or after they have split into smaller groups.

Having set up the washing line, issue the items of clothing to the groups and ask them to begin to hang out their washing in what they think is the correct order.

This activity is probably best run with two or three groups remaining in the main room rather than sending all the groups out into syndicate rooms. It can be difficult to move from room to room with a washing-line full of cardboard washing without various items falling off!

Monitoring

If all the groups are in the same room, you can easily wander around and listen and observe what is happening. Keep a mental or written note of any groups who seem to be heading off track. If you wish, you can intervene to help by asking questions to check out their rationale and giving advice to get them back on track.

In this activity, you could also suggest that they look at what the other groups are doing and check out their thoughts.

Reviewing

You can review this activity by getting each group to talk through their results, and see how they compare with the others. Any differences can be explored in more detail if necessary. You could also divide up the review so that each group talks about their first piece(s) of washing, then move on to discuss the second piece, and so on, with a different team explaining their results first. This ensures that each group gets a similar amount of time to give their explanations.

Examples of use

The Washing Line activity has been used successfully on a number of courses, using T-shirts and shorts. It tends to be one of the most popular of all the activities.

On one course it was used to produce a hierarchy of different types of assertive behaviour. The laminated cardboard T-shirts (about eight inches high) had the name of the type of assertion written on the front of the T-shirt (using WordArt). Beneath this was the definition. Examples of each type of assertion were printed onto cardboard shorts.

A similar approach was taken on a change management training event where different types of change were put into a hierarchy of difficulty to implement. As with the assertiveness activity, names and definitions were printed on T-shirts, and examples on shorts.

At the end of the day *after* this activity was carried out, with all the materials packed away, I asked the group what the types of change were called, and what the sequence was of least difficult to most difficult. Just about everybody joined in to reel off the names, in exactly the right order. Not a very scientific evaluation I know, but particularly rewarding none the less.

SUMMARY

HOW IT WORKS	**Trainer** • Set up room beforehand with washing lines (string) for each group • Issue groups with a set of cards that show information that can be placed into a hierarchy or sequence, printed as plain 'sheets' or as items of clothing (such as T-shirts and shorts) **Groups** • Sort cards into hierarchical order, and hang them on the line **Trainer** • Review the results, compare differences and similarities • Issue handout showing the information on the cards in the correct sequence
WHY IT WORKS	• Enables discussion with a lot of 'buzzing' movement, and physical manipulation • Can have added visual stimulation of irregular but recognizable shapes (T-shirts for example) – that make people smile!
PURPOSE AND PRINCIPLES	• Used to enable groups to actively identify actual or possible hierarchies, sequences, orders or levels of things • Works on similar principles to NDE Cards, with the added hierarchy element
PREPARATION	**Find suitable source material** • Use information that can be sorted into a definite hierarchy or sequence (easy to difficult/low to high and so on) **Produce the cards and other materials** • Cut out the clothing shapes you want and use these as a template to draw around the written information printed on cards of different colours, which can then be laminated and cut out • Aim for between four to ten items of clothing • Consider using WordArt and clip art to add visual interest • Consider using actual items of clothing • Obtain appropriate lengths of string, and sufficient numbers of pegs or clips • Produce a handout of the correct information in a similar styles or in table form
RUNNING	**Briefing** • Set up the room beforehand, and then explain the process and purpose of the activity • Keep all groups in same room **Monitoring** • Listen and observe. Intervene if necessary, and possibly allow groups to 'peek' at what the others are doing **Reviewing** • Ask each group to talk through their results, possibly about one item each in turn • Ask for comments from other groups. Explore differences and the reasoning behind the card placements, especially if different to suggested answers

Part 4
Games and Activity
Boards

Yes or No?

HOW IT WORKS

1   A card with a short case-study scenario, and a question on what could or should be done in relation to the scenario, is read out to all players.
2   Players consider what they would do (as managers for example) and indicate their answer to the question with a yes, no or depends card.
3   The reasoning behind the responses are discussed and the results recorded.
4   The results are reviewed and scored as necessary.

WHY IT WORKS

Yes or No? is a game that helps people become familiar with issues relating to organizational policies which might otherwise be quite tedious or dull to cover as a presentation.

The game provides an effective vehicle for discussion and debate and enables the free expression of viewpoints. The game allows serious issues to be raised and discussed in a light-hearted way. It is an activity that has its roots in the board game 'Scruples' where players are given ethical and moral dilemmas to consider and decide on what they would do.

PURPOSE AND PRINCIPLES

This game is highly effective in helping people become familiar with the *range* of policy areas that exist within the organization, and the *scope* of what the main policies cover.

The game allows people to consider real life or realistic scenarios and decide on what action to take. It can cover a whole range of policy areas such as:

- absence
- finance and procurement
- entertaining and acceptance of gifts
- work–life balance and flexible working
- equal opportunities and diversity
- travel and subsistence
- performance management
- recruitment and selection.

PREPARATION

Materials needed

To play this game you will need:

- sets of three cards with ,yes,, 'no' or 'depends' written on one card in each set
- a set of scenario cards
- a score/comment sheet
- instructions on how to play.

Producing the materials

What you write on the scenario cards will determine the mood of this activity. Policy issues can often be fairly dull, but with this game you can provide some unusual or bizarre examples within the scenarios, especially if they are true (but be aware of any confidentiality issues).

Two examples are shown in Figure A13.1 to illustrate the point. Scenario card number 1 raises the policy issue of work–life balance, and card number 2 raises a purchasing issue. The answers of course will vary depending on the organization's policy.

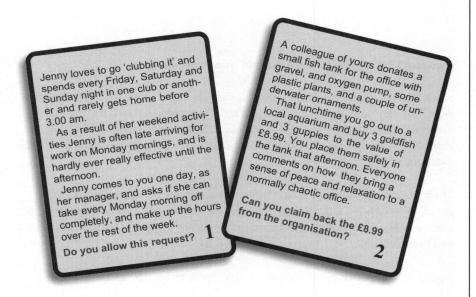

Jenny loves to go 'clubbing it' and spends every Friday, Saturday and Sunday night in one club or another and rarely gets home before 3.00 am.
As a result of her weekend activities Jenny is often late arriving for work on Monday mornings, and is hardly ever really effective until the afternoon.
Jenny comes to you one day, as her manager, and asks if she can take every Monday morning off completely, and make up the hours over the rest of the week.
Do you allow this request? **1**

A colleague of yours donates a small fish tank for the office with gravel, and oxygen pump, some plastic plants, and a couple of underwater ornaments.
That lunchtime you go out to a local aquarium and buy 3 goldfish and 3 guppies to the value of £8.99. You place them safely in the tank that afternoon. Everyone comments on how they bring a sense of peace and relaxation to a normally chaotic office.
Can you claim back the £8.99 from the organisation? **2**

Figure A13.1 Yes or No? – examples of cards

Yes or No? usually works well with between six and ten scenario cards for groups to consider. Try to get a range of scenarios to use, with one or two being fairly obvious, but also a few that would be 'borderline' cases – and one or two that seem to be too silly to be true – but are! Try also to get a relatively equal mix of yes, no, depends answers, or have at least one of each as a correct answer somewhere.

You will need to prepare an answer sheet to be used by each group. An example of how an answer sheet can look is shown below. Each group's responses should be recorded on it by placing ticks in the relevant yes/no/depends boxes. The 'reasons' box can be completed with a brief summary or trigger notes of the individual rationales.

SCENARIO	YES	NO	DE-PENDS	REASONS
1. **Clubber**	✓	✓ ✓	✓ ✓ ✓	OK if start time not essential. Not for that! No moral judgement.
2. **Fish tank**		✓ ✓ ✓	✓ ✓	Not proper purchase. Health and safety too. OK if approved by mana-
3. **Etc.**				
4. **Etc.**				
5.				

Figure A13.2 Yes or No? – example of a score card

It is advisable to prepare a completed answer sheet for your own reference as well. This can show the 'right' or 'most right' answers, and also the policies involved and where further information can be found. If the answer sheet contains enough relevant information like this, it can be issued as a handout to everybody.

The instructions on how to play the game can be written out as 'rules' of the game, to be handed out with the sets of cards and answer sheet. Make sure the rules are clear and concise. Produce a draft and test them out with others before you finalize them.

As a more competitive option, you could prepare to run the game as a competition between the different teams playing the game and therefore ask for consensus 'team answers' and give a score to every one the team gets right.

You will need to prepare a different kind of answer sheet if you want to run the game in this way, with a column to record whether the answer was correct and a total score box somewhere near the bottom of the page.

Note also that you can use this game as a more serious activity, without emphasizing the 'game' element of it. Serious and important scenarios could be used to explore groups' responses and views on issues such as welfare, discipline and poor performance policies and so on.

RUNNING THE ACTIVITY

The rules

Each player is given a set of three cards that have yes, no and depends written on them. These are kept face down in front of each player. In the middle of the table, also placed face down, are the scenario cards. Each of these cards contains one scenario relating to a particular policy or other issue.

The first scenario card is then turned over and the scenario read out loud to all the players. These cards also pose a question which all players must consider. The questions can all be answered by yes, no or depends.

After considering the question, each player then places a yes, no or depends card face down in front of them, depending on how they would deal with the scenario. When everyone is ready, the players turn over their cards and from this point their answers are discussed and debated. People are allowed to change their minds if they wish after hearing the views of others.

When the discussion has finished, one of the players completes the answer sheet. This will summarize the issue and record the number of people who said yes, no or depends. The reasoning behind the various answers can also be briefly noted for later reference.

Briefing

At the start, you will need to explain the purpose of the session in order to enable the participants to become familiar with the range and/or scope of some of the organization's policies.

You can then explain that it will be carried out by way of a game that will help achieve the familiarization.

At this point you can issue all of the materials that the groups need and simply ask them to read out the rules, check that everyone understands them and ask them to make a start when they are ready.

Monitoring

If you have a number of groups playing the game in the room, wander around as they are playing and listen to the conversations. They will invariably be useful to refer back to when you review the activity.

Reviewing

By the end of the game, all groups should have a completed answer sheet. When ready, you can review the game by asking each group to explain their thoughts on each of the scenarios in turn. You can then compare their responses with your 'right' answers and discuss any issues that may arise. After the review, issue the handouts and ensure everyone is OK with rationale of the 'right' answers before moving on.

EXAMPLE OF USE

Yes or No? has been used on induction training courses to provide an overview of the scope of human resources, finance, security and other policy areas of the organization. For this course, the group was split around a cabaret-style table arrangement, with four to six people at each table.

The two example scenario cards shown in Figure A13.1 were used in this particular activity, and one of the scenarios is based on a true event! This Yes or No? game used eight scenarios. Some of the scenarios were relatively obvious, but there were three or four that caused quite some debate, and a mixture of the yes/no/depends cards were put forward by the people in some groups for the same scenario.

On the 'fun-factor' side of things, this activity came out as being one of the most enjoyable. There was always a lot of debate and laughter in the room and there were also a lot of misconceptions demonstrated and dealt with.

Newer managers especially found it more difficult to deal with some of the more liberal aspects of the organization's policy. The 'clubbing' scenario for example had a correct 'depends' answer. If Jenny does not have a specified time of attendance, then her request is allowable under the organization's work–life balance policy (without any moral judgements being made about the reasons for the request). A number of new managers and staff with some preconceived ideas about managing and being managed found this quite surprising.

SUMMARY

HOW IT WORKS	• Game played by groups of two to six players (possibly more) • A scenario card with a question on what could be done is read out to all players • Players consider what they would do and indicate this with a yes/no or depends card • The reasoning behind the responses are discussed and the results recorded • The results are reviewed and scored as necessary
WHY IT WORKS	• Provides information about organizational policies in a much more engaging way than a traditional presentation • It can promote debate on serious issues in a light-hearted way • It works a little like the popular board game 'Scruples' which deals with moral and ethical dilemmas
PURPOSE AND PRINCIPLES	• Helps people become familiar with the range and scope of policy issues such as absence, finance and procurement, travel expenses • People consider real or realistic scenarios and decide on what action they would, should or could to take
PREPARATION	**Find suitable source material** • Obtain examples of real policy issues that have been dealt with in the past – can be serious or bizarre depending on requirements (consider confidentiality issues however) • Aim for a roughly even spread of yes, no, depends answers **Materials needed** • Sets of three cards for each player with yes/no/depends written on them • A set of scenario cards • An answer/score sheet • Instructions on how to play **Production** • Number the scenario cards and match the numbers with the answer/score sheets • Aim for between six to ten scenario cards across a range of policy topics – or specialize in just one or two
RUNNING	**Briefing** • Explain the purpose of the activity and the policy areas to be covered • Issue all materials and provide written or verbal instructions **Monitoring** • Listen and observe. Intervene only to clarify the rules **Reviewing** • Ask each group to talk through their results, possibly one scenario each in turn • Provide the correct answers as the review progresses and discuss any issues that may arise • Issue the handout with the scenarios and the correct answers at the end

True/False

Project Sponsor
Responsible for approving the project plan

Project Sponsor
Responsible for ensuring the completion of a discrete part of the project

Project Sponsor
Responsible for signing off the project when completed

TRUE   FALSE   TRUE

HOW IT WORKS

This is a game played with two teams of three or four players facing each other across a table.

1   One team then reads out three statements about a particular topic, written on a set of cards, and holds them up for the other team to read.
2   The other team then confer and place an appropriate true/false sign opposite each person holding the statements.
3   In turn, the statement cards are turned to reveal if the statement is true or false.
4   The teams then reverse roles for the next round.

WHY IT WORKS

A good 'buzz' can occur when people around two or more tables are playing the game. Even with just one table, an element of competition is likely to arise, whether intended or not, which can add some sparkle to the activity.

Any misconceptions about any of the topics can be identified in a non-threatening way, and getting an answer wrong is usually a trigger for 'ooohs' and 'aaaghs' and laughter, followed by the desire for an explanation.

PURPOSE AND PRINCIPLES

True/False works something like the old TV quiz show *Call My Bluff*. In this show, contestants were given three definitions to an obscure word from the Oxford English Dictionary, and had to try to identify the one correct definition after all three had been read out.

The game can help people acquire new knowledge, especially if it is in an area where there could be some surprising true answers or where are common misconceptions about what is true or not. It allows people to learn from each other during the discussions of what may be true or false. Those who 'know' can explain the reasons to those who do not.

True/False works well with subject matter like roles and responsibilities, where different people have different responsibilities – a good example is project management, where there might be different responsibilities for the project's sponsors, managers and stage managers. For this project management example, you could use cards like those in Figure A14.1.

Project Sponsor Responsible for approving the project plan	Project Sponsor Responsible for ensuring the completion of a discrete part of the project	Project Sponsor Responsible for signing off the project when completed

Figure A14.1 True/False – examples of cards

For this example set of three cards, numbers 1 and 3 would be true, and number 2 would be false.

PREPARATION

The only materials you need to prepare for this game are the cards and the true/false signs.

You will need cards with statements for each team. The number of cards and statements will be up to you, but the three sets of three has proven to be a good number – not too many, nor too few. Each set of three statements should be printed on different coloured card to make it easier to identify them.

For the two teams to play, each team will need a set of cards to read out and display, so with the three sets of three, you will need a total of 18 cards. If this is too many for the subject matter you have, you could still run the game with a total of six cards per team.

Project Sponsor **Responsible for en-suring the comple-tion of a discrete part of the project**	Project Sponsor Responsible for ensuring the completion of a discrete part of the project **FALSE**
FRONT	**BACK**

Figure A14.2 True/ False – front and back

When preparing the cards, it is usually best to print on both sides, so that the reverse side can simply be twisted around to reveal the correct True/False answer. If you print the statement on the back of the card as well, the person holding it up will be able to read off what is written as they hold up the card so the front of it can be seen by the team opposite, as in the example below.

If you wish, you could have points scored for every correct answer and add an element of competition. If you want to do this, you may also need to produce a scoring sheet to be completed.

RUNNING THE ACTIVITY

The rules

The True/False game needs to have at least two teams of three or four players facing each other, usually across a table. Each team has a set of cards with statements written on the front. As I mentioned earlier, having three sets of three cards per team usually works well.

To start the game, the first team reads out all three of their first set of statements and also displays them to the team opposite. Usually, one card is read out by one person and held up for the other team to see. Another person then reads out and displays the second card, and then the third person reads and displays the third card.

When all three cards have been read out and displayed, the team opposite has to confer and decide which statements they think are true, and which false. Once decided, they can use the three true/false signs and place them opposite the person who has read out the statement to indicate which is which.

When the true/false cards have been placed in the agreed order, the people holding up the cards reveal which statements are true, and which are false. This is done by twisting the card around and showing the statement and the answer that is printed on the reverse.

Briefing

The True/False game requires the careful explanation of what it is for and how to run it. Be clear when you explain the rules, but once they are up and running let them get on with it as much as possible.

Monitoring

As you listen and observe the activity, listen out for any incorrect answers. You will need to decide whether to intervene immediately or wait until the end.

If a team gets an answer wrong, they might ask you for an immediate explanation. Use your judgement. If teams are generally getting the same answers wrong, you could give a brief explanation if asked and also a more detailed explanation when you review the game at the end.

If you have a number of groups playing this game in the same room, you will also need to check on how quickly they are progressing. Some groups may well be quicker than others. If this is the case, you can perhaps discuss any questions or issues raised with any group that has finished, then raise the points again when you review with all the groups at the end. You can also check whether other groups had similar queries.

Reviewing

When you do review the game, you can ask questions like:

- How obvious were the answers?
- Any surprises?
- How much debate was needed before the team agreed an answer?
- Which ones did you get wrong?
- How clear are you on the issue now?

You can then discuss any questions or issues that arise. It will be important to ensure that any group that got an incorrect answer are clear about the reasoning behind the correct answer.

EXAMPLE OF USE

True/False has been used on courses to cover the roles and responsibilities of different job grades within an organization, and also to cover the roles and responsibilities of different people in order to meet the standards set for the Investors in People (IiP) award.

To use the IiP cards as an example, one set of three cards related to the actions or knowledge that senior managers, line managers and individuals would need to demonstrate in order to meet the standards. One team read out the statements, and another positioned the true/false signs depending on whether they felt the statements were true or false.

This activity provided participants with the knowledge of the actual roles of the main players in the IiP process – which included them. There were one or two shocks when some people, especially managers, realized what they were expected to do. When used for this kind of purpose, True/False can bring some important points home to people that they did either not know (or what they chose not to acknowledge) beforehand.

SUMMARY

HOW IT WORKS	• Game played with two teams of three to four players facing each other across a table • One team then reads out statements written on a set of cards, and holds them up for the other team to read • The other team then confer and place an appropriate true/false nameplate opposite each person holding the statements • In turn, the statement cards are turned to reveal if the statement is true or false • The teams then reverse roles for the next round
WHY IT WORKS	• A good 'buzz' can occur when people around two or more tables are playing the game • Any misconceptions can be identified and rectified in a non-threatening way • An element of competition, whether intended or not, can add a sparkle to the activity
PURPOSE AND PRINCIPLES	• Works on a similar principle to the old *Call My Bluff* TV quiz show • People learn from each other during the discussions of what may be true or false • Can work well with topics where there can be misconceptions about what is true or not
PREPARATION	**Find suitable source material** • Can work well with topics like 'roles and responsibilities', but many topics will be suitable as long as sufficient numbers of true and false statements can be made **Produce the cards and other materials** • Three sets of three cards per team usually work well. This requires 18 statements in total but this can be easily reduced • Print the statements on both sides of the card so they can be read from the back whilst the front is displayed • In large print or WordArt, also show 'True' or 'False' on the reverse of each card as appropriate, so it can be seen easily when turned around
RUNNING	**Briefing** • Explain the purpose of the activity and provide written or verbal instructions • You could prepare a mock set of cards to demonstrate the process if necessary **Monitoring** • Listen and observe for any common misconceptions being aired. You can intervene at this stage, or wait until the review • You may get asked directly for an explanation. You can answer, but then explain, but then raise the issue again in the general review **Reviewing** • The review will mainly consist of asking questions about player's reactions to the answers – any surprises? • Ensure any common misconceptions are dealt with, and that everyone is clear of the correct information by the end • Issue any relevant handouts

What Am I?

HOW IT WORKS

A stack of cards is placed face down in the centre of the table. On each card is either a word or a brief description of a skill relevant to the subject matter of the training.

1   Each person takes turns in picking the top card from the stack and showing it to the rest of the group. The person picking the card is not allowed to see what is written on it.

2   The rest of the group then have to provide clues to the person who has picked the card to enable them to identify and state the key word or skill that is on it. (The group, however, is not allowed to use the actual key word(s) which are written on the card.) If the card relates to a skill, one or more people in the group have to *demonstrate* the skill in order to provide the clue.

WHY IT WORKS

What Am I? is used mainly as a way of evaluating learning, although it could also be used as a learning activity in its own right. It can help evaluate the learning of knowledge and also some types of skill. Because it is based on a party game, there can be a great element of fun to it. It can also be a very speedy way of evaluating, and also consolidating the learning achieved.

You can use What Am I? to test almost any form of knowledge as long as there is a word, phrase or statement that can be described, defined or demonstrated.

The use of demonstrations allows the practice of some skills to be carried out. For example, the group in front of the person holding a card with 'Summarizing' written on it could demonstrate this between them to enable the card-holder to identify this particular kind of active listening skill.

PURPOSE AND PRINCIPLES

What Am I? is based on the game where someone holds a card (with for example a famous person's name written on it) to their forehead with their finger, with the words facing the other players. The other players have to provide clues as to whom the famous person is, without saying their actual name. The person holding the card has to identify and state who they think the famous person is.

What Am I? works something like this, but using cards with words, statements or information relating to the course content. It usually works well with teams of four to six people, preferably in separate syndicate rooms.

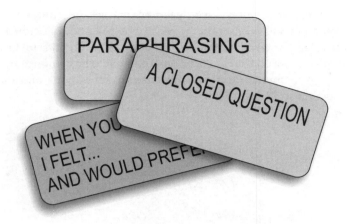

PREPARATION

Preparation for What Am I? is relatively straightforward. All you need is the cards with the relevant words or statements written on them.

If you are using it for skills demonstrations, make sure that the skill is actually one that can be demonstrated quickly and easily by the teams. Aim to produce between nine and twelve cards so that each person in a team of three and four people can try to identify three cards each in turn. You will need one set of questions for each team.

If you wish, you can produce the cards on slips smaller than A4 or A5, and use the finger-to-the-forehead way of displaying the card so that the holder cannot see it.

You will find that some words can only test knowledge and cannot be demonstrated as a skill, whilst other words can be described or defined *and* demonstrated. You will need to either let the teams do *either* (define *or* demonstrate) or note on the card itself whether it *must* be demonstrated. You could have one colour of cards for definitions and descriptions, and another colour for demonstrations.

In the example of the 'Closed Question' card above, either teams could give a clue along the lines of 'It's a question requiring a yes/no or single-word answer', or someone could demonstrate it by saying to the card-holder, 'What kind of question is this?' and then asking another team member the question: 'Do you like cheese?'

When a card is revealed to the team, they should be given a minute or two to prepare their clues, and a little more time if they need to prepare a demonstration.

The game will be over when all the cards have been identified correctly, or when the team is down to a final one or two that cannot be identified.

RUNNING THE ACTIVITY

Briefing

You will need to brief the teams about how the game works, and its purpose of evaluating what has been learned.

Split the group into teams of three or four people and either deal out the cards to each person or simply place them face down in the middle of the table for each person to pick one up when it is their turn. This way, if the person holding the card fails to identify the words correctly, the card can be returned to the bottom of the pile.

Monitoring

Depending on numbers of players, you as the trainer could be the card-holder who has to identify what's on the cards, and the group could provide all of the clues and demonstrations. This way you will be able to observe everything, although you will need to have sufficient numbers of trainers to work with each group.

Even if you are not participating by being the card-holder, you could walk around to see the different groups and intervene if you need to. You could, for example ask questions to help the team clarify their thoughts before giving a demonstration. You may also need to remind the groups to keep their voices down and beware of giving away the answer whilst conferring or planning their demonstration.

Reviewing

This again should be relatively straightforward. If you are present during the activity, you will see if the team is struggling with any particular concepts. If there are any issues outstanding, you can recap on them and discuss as necessary during the review.

If you were not there, you could ask if there were any cards that could not be identified, and why. If there are still some outstanding gaps in knowledge or understanding, you can make the necessary interventions to fill them.

EXAMPLE OF USE

What Am I? has been used on communication skills courses to evaluate and develop the knowledge and skills relating to questioning and listening skills in particular. To evaluate knowledge gain there were cards with the names of the particular types of question, and the groups were allowed to choose to either offer clues or demonstrate the asking of the questions. A similar approach was taken with the listening-skills element of the course.

The activity showed that the method worked well to consolidate the knowledge gained, and what had been learned about putting the knowledge into practice.

Whilst the card-holder had to demonstrate their knowledge by responding to the clues or demonstrations, the people providing the clues and demonstrations were also displaying their knowledge and understanding.

It was also found, however, that some participants were more comfortable than others in providing the clues and demonstrations. Those who were more reserved or reflective tended to let the more gregarious and active people get on with it. A way around this was either to split the clue-giving/demonstrating group into pairs to deal with one card at a time. Another option was to simply allow the more reflective individuals to participate, or not, as they wished.

On one occasion this activity was used too early on a training event, with insufficient explanation given about it, and it was a struggle to get it to work. The participants had yet to become relaxed or confident enough to go with it in the way it was intended. It works better during the later stages of an event, when the group are more comfortable with each other and the facilitator. The logistics also needed to be explained fully, especially in the areas of how the roles would be rotated, so that everyone could be a card-holder, and what was to happen to any cards that could not be identified by the card holder (that is, putting them back to the bottom of the pile).

SUMMARY

HOW IT WORKS	• The game works best with teams of four to six people, preferably in separate syndicate rooms • A stack of cards is placed face down in the centre of a table. On each card is a word, statement or a type of skill relevant to the subject matter of the training • Each player takes a card in turn and shows it to the rest of the group, without being able to see it themselves • The rest of the group then have to provide clues, or demonstrate the skill, to enable the player holding the card to identify what is written on it • The game is over when all the cards, or as many as possible, have been correctly identified
WHY IT WORKS	• Based on a party game, it is a fun method that can be used to test almost any form of knowledge, without the feeling that anyone is actually being tested
PURPOSE AND PRINCIPLES	• A game that is used to evaluate knowledge and possibly skills learned during an event • Based on the game where someone holds a word printed on a card to their forehead and others provide clues to help them identify the word on the card, without actually using the word on the card • Can possibly be used as a learning method in its own right, and not just for evaluation
PREPARATION	**Find suitable source material** • You can use almost any type of material as long as there are some key words or concepts that are important to be known and can be described, defined or demonstrated **Produce the cards and other materials** • Produce between nine and twelve cards for each of three to four players to take three turns each to hold up a card • You will need one set for each team • Produce on any card from A5–A4 size, or smaller if you want to use the 'finger to the forehead' approach • Can have different coloured card for words that have to be demonstrated by the group
RUNNING	**Briefing** • Explain the purpose of the activity. As an evaluation exercise for example • Explain the rules of the game and how it will work **Monitoring** • Keep an eye out for any words or concepts that cannot be identified, and note them for the review • You made need to remind the group to keep their voices down when conferring about what to do • You could use questioning to help the group clarify their thoughts before giving a demonstration **Reviewing** • Recap on any cards that could not be identified, and clarify as necessary to fill any gaps in knowledge or understanding

The Evaluation Game

HOW IT WORKS

1 Teams throw a die to move around a board. Depending on where they land, they either answer a question or demonstrate a skill for others to identify.

2 Correct answers and successful demonstrations are rewarded by the player keeping the relevant question card, which counts as a 'point'. Bonus points can also be earned.

3 The game continues until either all the cards have been used or the agreed time limit or number of rounds is reached. The team with the highest points total wins.

WHY IT WORKS

Playing the Evaluation Game at the end of a training course is an excellent way of checking out what has been learned in a light-hearted and enjoyable way.

It also works as a means of consolidating and recapping on the content of a learning event.

The game provides an entertaining means of rounding off a training event, working on a similar basis to the highly popular trivia quiz games.

PURPOSE AND PRINCIPLES

The Evaluation Game is an activity which you can use to evaluate the learning of both knowledge and skills. It works on a similar principle to trivia type quiz games, but this game has more to it than just the asking and answering of questions.

The Evaluation Game is best played by three or four teams of three or four people. It involves the answering of questions on the various topics of the training event, and also the demonstration and identification of relevant skills.

Participants roll a die to move around a board of coloured squares, answering questions or demonstrating skills as they go.

Each coloured square on the Evaluation Game board represents a different topic covered on the training event. For example on a 'Management Communication' course the questions and demonstrations for each topic could be divided between the colours as follows:

- red – listening
- blue – questioning
- green – feedback
- yellow – influencing styles and assertiveness
- orange (the four corners) – the team can choose *any* colour).

Of course, you can use any colours of your choice, and you could have one colour representing more than one topic if necessary.

PREPARATION

Materials needed

To run the Evaluation Game you will need:

- the board
- question/demonstration cards – between ten and fifteen in total for each colour
- a marker/token for each team
- cards or disks for bonus points
- one die.

Once made, the board can be used on any number of training events, with different sets of questions for different events.

Making the board

Making the board for the Evaluation Game is even easier than making the board for the Room 2 Room activity (Activity 17).

An A3 sized board is made up from two A4 sheets of card. If you have access to a colour printer, you can draw up the squares in Microsoft Word and give them whatever colour fills you wish.

To make the squares, use the 'rectangle' tool from the drawing toolbar. Right click on it and from the Format AutoShape menu, click on 'Size' and enter the measurement you want.

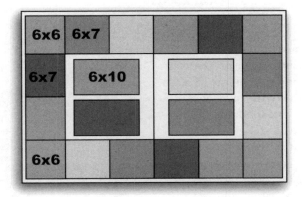

Figure A16.1 The Evaluation Game – board measurements

The rectangle/square sizes you will need for two A4 halves to make up an A3 board are:

- four squares of 6 × 6 cm of the same colour for the corners;
- three rectangles of 6 × 7 cm for *each* of the other colours;
- one rectangle of 6 × 10 cm for each colour, except the colour of the corners, for the inside of the board (see Figure A16.1).

If you do not have access to a colour printer (or you want to conserve your ink!) all you need to do is cut out the rectangles and squares you need from coloured card and stick them onto the two sheets of A4, leaving a border around the edge that you can leave or trim as you wish.

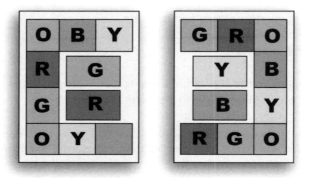

Figure A16.2 The Evaluation Game – board colours

Producing the question cards

If using Microsoft Word to produce the cards, make sure you have your template for them centred on the page so that you can print the front, and then put the card through again to print 'Quest' or 'Demo' as appropriate on the back. To fit nicely on the centre rectangles of the board, the cards should measure about 5.5 × 9 cm.

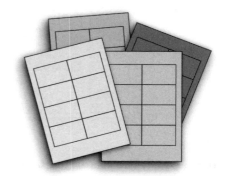

There are two types of question card to be produced if you are going to use the 'Quest' and 'Demo' approach. The question cards are the easiest to produce. These should be based on important learning points covered during the training event. Avoid asking questions on obscure or inconsequential topics. Also try to avoid making them too easy or too difficult.

It is good practice to test them out on people to ensure that they are not vague or ambiguous.

When preparing the demo cards you might find it useful to provide the actual words for the team to read out immediately before carrying out the demonstration. This will ensure that all parties are aware of what is required. The examples in Figure A16.3 show what the demonstrating team should say.

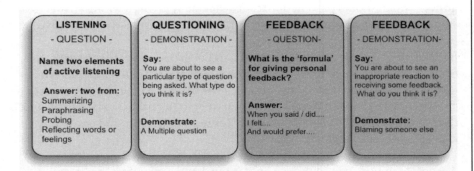

Figure A16.3 The Evaluation Game – examples of questions

When the board and the cards have been produced, you should then draft a clear explanation of the rules that you want to apply. Test the rules out with people as well before you go live with the game.

RUNNING THE ACTIVITY

The rules

Each team in turn throws a die and moves a marker or token around the perimeter of the board in any direction they choose. If the marker lands on a red square, then the top question card on the red pile is picked up. Each card will either ask a direct question, or it will ask for a particular skill to be demonstrated. Points and bonuses are available depending on the answers and outcomes.

The question cards are placed face down in piles on the appropriate coloured rectangle on the inside of the board. They are printed on the reverse with either 'Quest' or 'Demo'.

A quest card will have a straightforward question. It is picked up and read out by the team *to the left* of the team whose turn it is, who then have to answer the question if they can. If they answer correctly, the card is given to them and will count as a point. If they answer incorrectly, the card is returned to the bottom of the pile from which it came.

A demo card will require the team that has thrown the die to pick up the card themselves, ask the question printed on the card, and then carry out the required demonstration to the team *on their left*.

If the team to the left answer the question correctly after seeing the demonstration, *they* are awarded a *bonus point* card or disk. The team who carried out the demonstration would then keep the question card as a point – and *also* take a bonus point. (In this way both teams will gain from a correct answer, which should prevent one team deliberately giving a wrong answer to stop the other team from scoring!)

If the team to the left do not identify what is being demonstrated correctly, the card is to be returned to the bottom of the relevant pile. As an option, if teams do not get a question or demonstration answer correct, it could be passed on to another team to answer. If you use the rule whereby a card has to be returned to the bottom of the pack, it will eventually come around again, and one team or another may get it right.

As another option, you could also omit using demo cards altogether if you just wanted to test the learning of knowledge. You might also be able to devise different or additional ways of testing the knowledge and skill, or other ways of scoring points.

The end of the game will occur when one of the following occurs:

- There are no more cards to be answered.
- There is no more time.
- It has been agreed to end the game after a set number of rounds, for example five or six.

The winners will be the team with the most question/demo/bonus cards at the end of the game. You may want to consider awarding some prizes!

Briefing

If you have produced a set of rules, you could just explain the purpose of the activity (evaluation) to the teams, issue them with the rules and let them get on with it. Oral explanations of the rules by the trainer tend to result in a lot of questions being asked, and you can easily get bogged down in 'But what if...?' questions.

Just issuing the written rules at the start, with a brief introduction tends to work best. There always seems to someone in the team who is willing to pick up the rules, read out enough for the game to get started, and then refer to them when necessary as the game progresses.

Monitoring

If all goes well, and the players are happy with the rules and how to play the game, you should be able to just let them get on with it. All you may need to do is observe how things are going. If the Evaluation Game is used as an activity to round off a training course, it will be preferable to avoid any kind of intervention unless absolutely necessary (or just to clarify any of the rules).

You can, however, seek to be aware of any areas where there appear to be some gaps in the learning or grave misunderstandings. These will need to be dealt with in a review.

Reviewing

As this is meant to be a final evaluation activity, the review should not need to be in-depth. Perhaps just filling in any gaps as mentioned above.

You can, however, use the end of the activity as an opportunity to highlight and recognize the amount of knowledge and skills that have been learned during the event.

EXAMPLE OF USE

The Evaluation Game was originally developed as an activity to finish off a trainer-training programme, and covered the interpersonal skills required of trainers, like those listed at the start of this chapter (listening, questioning, giving feedback, and so on).

At the end of this particular trainer-training event, each participant was provided with one-to-one feedback from the trainer about their own skills and development as trainers. This meant that if there were two trainers, each managing a feedback session, the rest of the group would need to be kept occupied until everyone had had their turn. Hence, this game was developed to be almost self-running. In practice therefore it was never monitored or reviewed because the trainers were in other rooms providing feedback to individual trainee-trainers.

On one occasion, the trainers delivering the event may not have explained the purpose of the Evaluation Game in the manner expected. It was reported to me later that the participants were unhappy because they knew all the answers!

SUMMARY

HOW IT WORKS	• Teams throw a die to move around a board, and either answer a question or demonstrate a skill for others to identify • Correct answers are rewarded by keeping the relevant card which counts as a 'point'. Bonus points can also be earned • The game continues until either all the cards have been used, or the agreed time limit or number of rounds is reached and the team with the highest points total wins
WHY IT WORKS	• When played at the end of a learning event it enables the evaluation of much of the course content for the trainer's benefit • It also provides a means of consolidating at recapping the knowledge and skills covered on the event for the learner's benefit • It provides a light-hearted means of rounding off a training event • Works on a similar basis to the highly popular trivia quiz games
PURPOSE AND PRINCIPLES	• A board game that can be used to evaluate the learning of both knowledge and skills • It can be played by three or four teams of three to five players • Each coloured square on the board represents one or more topics covered on the event • Involves teams answering questions on the course content, and demonstrating skills via the use of 'quest' cards and 'demo' cards
PREPARATION	**Materials** • The Board • Question/demonstration cards • Bonus cards • A marker/token for each team • One die **Production** • Make the board – A3 size from two sheets of A4 card and squares/rectangles from coloured card • Produce the quest and demo cards; they should fit within the rectangles in the centre of the board • Quest cards should be on important items of knowledge, and demo cards should be skills that can be demonstrated. Test them out before going live • Print the actual words to be read out for the demo cards • Draft the rules and check them out for clarity
RUNNING	**Briefing** • Explain the evaluative purpose of the activity and issue the rules. Avoid explaining them all verbally, but be prepared to clarify if necessary **Monitoring** • It is probably best to avoid any kind of intervention unless to clarify any of the rules during the game • You can listen out for evidence of any remaining gaps in the learning, however **Reviewing** • Fill any remaining gaps as noted during the monitoring • If you have not monitored in any depth, you can simply ask the teams if there are still any outstanding issues to be clarified

Room 2 Room

HOW IT WORKS

1   Groups of around five or six people work their way around a board showing a floor plan of different rooms. Each room represents a different element of the topic or course that you are running.
2   Each player places a token in one of the rooms and when their turn comes, opens a particular envelope to read out the instructions on how to carry out an activity. Each activity will be something the activities described throughout this book.
3   After a brief introduction to each room by the trainer, the activity is carried out by the groups and the results reviewed before moving on to the next room and topic.

WHY IT WORKS

Room 2 Room allows teams of people to work together semi-autonomously, and is best used in conjunction with some of the other activities described in this book. People work their way from 'room to room', carrying out a different activity for each room visited. You can use Room 2 Room as the framework for a half- to one-day training event.

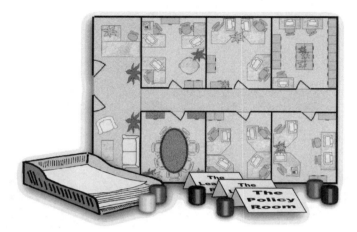

As it involves a board and various items of equipment, the activity has the look and feel of a board game. It can therefore have all the connotations that go with it in people's minds. It can invoke the times of friends and family gathering together and playing a game that is enjoyable and perhaps with a hint of friendly competition.

PURPOSE AND PRINCIPLES

The Room 2 Room activity provides a structure for a range of other activities. It is an activity that also promotes people working together in teams, and provides a focal point for people's attention and interest.

The main element of the activity is the board, which looks a little like the board for the detective board game of 'Cluedo', with a number of different rooms. Each room will represent a different element of the topic or course that you are running.

PREPARATION

Materials needed

- The board (one per team/table).
- A set of nameplates or cards to show the name of each room.
- A set of markers or tokens to show which person will be in charge of which room.

- An in-tray (one per team/table).
- A set of materials and instructions in which the activities for each room are to be placed.
- A set of envelopes, labelled with the name of each room, to be placed in the in-trays.

Figure A17.1 shows a board with six rooms and an (optional) entrance and reception area on the far left, so this will need six room nameplates, six markers and six activities in the six envelopes in the in-tray.

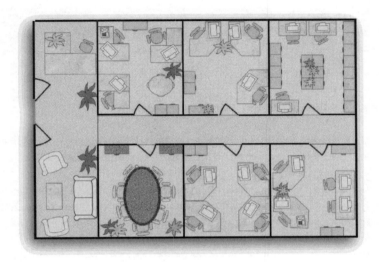

Figure A17.1 Room 2 Room – floor plan

For the Room 2 Room activity to work effectively, you need at least four topics to be covered, and thus at least four rooms. The topics you choose can vary greatly. You could have all of the envelope activities based around a single subject, such as assertiveness or leadership. Alternatively, you could have a number of very different topics, with just the common factor of the board to give them a structure.

If you make up a board of six rooms, you could have four rooms for the main topics, and use the other two for an introductions activity at the start and an evaluation activity at the end.

Making the board

This is much easier than you might think. All you need is:

- a PC or laptop with Microsoft Word;
- a colour printer;
- some sheets of A4 card or paper (white or coloured);

- two sheets of A3 card or paper (white or coloured) per board;
- if possible. an A3 laminator (or you can get A3 sheets laminated quite inexpensively in many high street photographic printing outlets).

Within the Microsoft Word AutoShapes menu (under 'More AutoShapes' > 'Office layout') you will find shapes of desks, chairs, tables, computers, plants, doors and other office furniture. Some examples are shown in Figure A17.2.

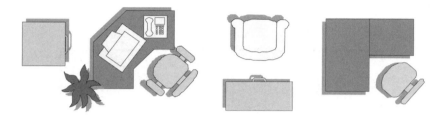

Figure A17.2 Room 2 Room – Office AutoShapes

All you then need to do is draw some rectangles to make up the floor plan of the rooms, and populate them with the office furniture AutoShapes.

If you use MS Word and draw two rectangles (for rooms) on A4 paper size, you can get the size of each room to be just under A5 size. This allows for six rooms, with extra space for the reception area, and the corridor down the centre.

Then you need to print the A4 sheets (possibly onto coloured paper) cut out the rooms and the reception area and physically paste them onto two sheets of A3 paper (see Figure A17.3).

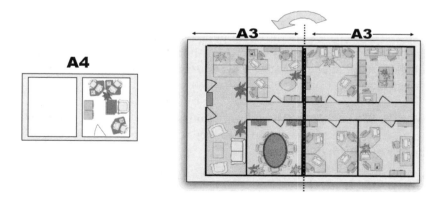

Figure A17.3 Room 2 Room – making the board

When laminated, the A3 sheets can be taped down the centre with clear tape, front and back, so the whole board can be folded in half. A board which is the size of two A3 paper sheets is ideal for tables that can seat around six people.

If you use larger or smaller tables, you can of course make larger or smaller boards. They do take some time to make, but once done and laminated, you can use them over and over again. Of course, if you have other drawing programmes with A3 colour-printing capabilities. The time and effort needed may be reduced drastically.

Not printing any room names on the board itself, and printing them on the folded nameplates instead, means that you can be flexible in the topics you cover when using the Room 2 Room board. It also means that you can use the same board for a number of training events covering different subjects.

Activities for each room

As mentioned already, you can use a range of different activities and games within the Room 2 Room method. Aim to have each room activity last about 20–30 minutes, followed by a 10–15-minute review.

Each activity will need instructions and any required materials. If you provide written instructions there is less verbal explaining for you to do. Two or three copies of the instructions might be required for each envelope. One can be read out loud by the person in charge, and another one or two will allow others to read them, and refer back to them during the activity if necessary.

Running the activity

The activity works best if the groups of participants can sit around tables with the board in the centre. The board is then set out on each table along with the in-tray containing all the envelopes, which in turn contain the instructions and any materials that will fit inside. (You can issue any other materials that will not fit into the envelopes separately when necessary.)

The nameplates or cards with the names of each room are then placed on the board, in each of the rooms. The markers are placed at one end of the board, or, as in the example board on the previous page, they can be placed in the reception area.

Briefing, monitoring and reviewing – the overall process

Once everything is set up on the tables, the process is then as follows:

1   You introduce the board and all the other materials and equipment, and explain the process and purpose of the activity.
2   You ask each person to pick a marker and place it in one of the rooms. This is the room that they will be 'in charge of' when the time comes.
3   You introduce the topic to be covered by the first room, and ask the person who is in charge of that room to open the relevant envelope and

read out the instructions. The instructions are then to be carried out as a team activity.

4   When all the teams at each table have finished the first activity, you review their results and discuss any issues raised etc.

5   You then introduce the second room and ask the next person in charge to read out the instructions within the next envelope. On completion, this activity is reviewed, and then you move on to the third room, and so on until every room has been visited and all the activities have been carried out.

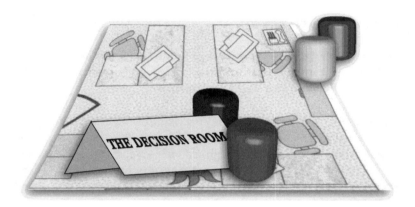

EXAMPLE OF USE

Room 2 Room has been used as the basis for a half-day induction training event. The board had six rooms, and each room was used in a very similar way to that described below.

Room 1 – the intros room

People introduce themselves to each other around their table individually or introduce someone on their table to everyone else in the room.

Room 2 – the unit room

A Category Card activity (see Activity 7) in which descriptions of the work of the various departments (units) in the organization have to be placed under the relevant name of each unit. People are also asked to expand upon the card description for their own unit, and offer some more information about their particular role and any issues that their unit is currently dealing with.

Room 3 – the plan room

An Info Hunt activity (see Activity 4) in which the groups complete a question sheet relating to the current business plans and vision of the organization. A copy of the organization's objectives and business plans was used as the basis for the questionnaire.

Room 4 – the roles room

A True/False game (see Activity 14) to help people understand the roles and responsibilities of staff of various job grades (executive, support, managerial and so on) within the organization.

Room 5 – the policy room

A Yes or No? game (see Activity 13) to highlight some of the main human resources, purchasing and travel and subsistence policies, and identify where additional information can be found when needed.

Room 6 – the wrap-up room

Groups were to write up on the flipchart their key learning points from the event, ask any outstanding questions and finally complete a course evaluation sheet.

Of course, you could always have the evaluation game as your final room activity!

NOT JUST ROOMS

The Room 2 Room activity board is just one way of structuring a training event or session. The same principle can be used in other ways if you have the graphic design (or hand-drawing) capabilities. For example, you could apply a similar approach and use concepts such as a treasure island, using a map of an island divided into different regions to represent different topics such as 'Feedback Bay', 'Communication Cove' or the 'The Jungle of Negotiation'. You can apply similar approaches to utilize themes like a mountain climbing expedition, or a river or train journey. The only limitation is your imagination!

SUMMARY

HOW IT WORKS	• Groups of around five or six people work their way around a board showing a floor plan of different rooms. Each room represents a different element of the topic or course that you are running • Each player places their token in one of the rooms and each in turn, opens a particular envelope to read out the instructions and begin the learning activity
WHY IT WORKS	• It allows groups to work together semi-autonomously • It has the look and feel of a board game, with the connotations that go with it, such as an enjoyable 'get together' and perhaps a hint of friendly competition
PURPOSE AND PRINCIPLES	• It provides a structure for a range of other activities • It provides a focal point for people's attention and interest • It can be used as a framework for a complete half to one-day event
PREPARATION	**Materials** • The board (one per group/table) • A set of nameplates or cards for each room • A set of markers or tokens that each group member places in one of the rooms • An in-tray • A set of instructions and materials inside envelopes on which the name of each room is written, to be placed in the in-tray **Production** • Make the board – two sheets of A3 card or paper • Can use office furniture AutoShapes in MS Word to make the floor plans • Prepare the materials and instructions for the activities to be placed in the envelopes (include at least two copies of the instructions in each envelope) • Aim to have each room activity lasting about 20–30 minutes, and then allow for a 10–15 minute review • Produce nameplates with the names (topics) for each room, stemming from the course content • You will need at least four topics to be covered, and thus at least four 'rooms' on the board
RUNNING	**Briefing** • Explain the purpose of the board and how it will be used • Introduce the topic of each room so that all groups are working on the same activity at the same time **Monitoring** • Keep an eye on the timings and the relative speeds of the groups. Some may need to be prompted. Fast finishers could be asked to consider other issues related to the topic • Note any issues that arise and discuss them in the review if relevant to everybody **Reviewing** • Review each activity before moving on and introducing the next one • Ask different groups to start first when presenting their activity results to help achieve an even spread of contributions from each group

Conclusion

Using Activity-Based Training

ACTIVITY-BASED SOLUTIONS

All of the activity-based methods described in this book originally started out as individual solutions to individual problems. For example:

- Info Hunt (Activity 4) was developed as a way of getting some long and complex policy information across to people, not in order that they should be able to remember every detail, but in order to make them aware of the scope and content of it, and *where* to find the detailed information when needed in the future.
- NDE Cards and Traffic Lights (Activities 8 and 9) were developed as a way of making the delivery of a session on questioning skills more active and engaging.
- The Evaluation Game was developed to provide something useful and enjoyable to do whilst the trainers provided one-to-one feedback to the participants.

Only afterwards was it discovered that the principles behind the individual solutions for particular sessions, could be applied to other sessions as well. The hierarchy element of Washing Line (Activity 12) could be used for establishing the relative difficulties of different types of change, as well as different types of assertiveness. Names, definitions and examples could be applied to many more things than just types of question.

It is my hope therefore that you will be able to examine some of the training sessions which you deliver and apply some of the activity-based methods to them. I will stick my neck out here and say that there is not one straight 'input' session on any topic that cannot be transformed into a more interesting activity. When you get used to working with activity-based methods, you may well find that when you look at an 'input' session in a training module, an appropriate activity just jumps straight out at you!

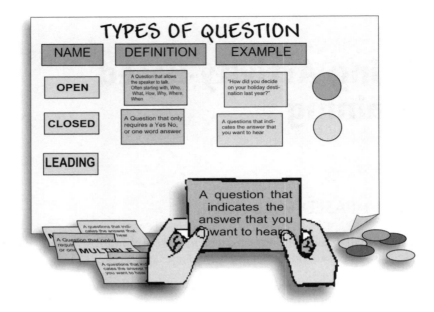

You may also find that you will be constantly looking for new 'problems' on which to apply an activity-based solution. This of course leads to the possibility of inventing more and more activity-based methods. I have devised a few, but there must be many more just waiting to be developed!

INTRODUCING ACTIVITY-BASED TRAINING

There are a few issues that you may face when trying to introduce activity-based training. These relate to introducing it to an organization, and then introducing it to groups of learners.

Introducing to the organization

You may need to negotiate with any decision-makers about introducing activity-based training methods within the organization. The benefits should be easily identified. If you get the go-ahead you can then consider how you can introduce it. One way is to do it gradually over a period of time and identify suitable sessions to transform as you go along. Alternatively you can introduce it in one go for a particular course and transform most of the sessions before launching it as a new event. One or two pilot sessions would be worth considering as you can then see how the participants react to the new approach. Much will also depend on how much time you have to design and produce the materials.

Introducing to learners

One of the major concerns about introducing activity-based methods is that the learners will not accept them. This is especially true of the more game-like activities. When trying out a new activity, I was always anxious that it would be judged as being too trivial or childish. At first I was surprised that no such comments were made, but now I can honestly say that the only reactions I have had have been positive. Various methods have been used with various groups both at home and abroad, at different job grades and levels, and there have been no complaints at all about trivialization or childishness.

Perhaps it could be put down to the fact that, on the whole, people are people, and people on the whole prefer to be relaxed and have fun while they are learning. No one has ever said anything like 'Actually I much prefer it when the trainer talks us through a large number of PowerPoint slides'!

Having said this, there are some things that you can do to help introduce the methods to learners so that they do not come as too great a shock. Some of these things are:

- Mention at the start of the event that some new methods are going to be used, and they have been designed to combine serious learning with serious fun.
- If you usually set some learning 'ground rules' at the start of an event, include a ground rule of something like: 'Be open to new ways of learning'.
- If you are using an activity-based method for the first time, say so. Tell the learners that they are going to be the first people to experience the new approach, and that you would appreciate their feedback at the end.
- After you have run the activity, you could also tell the group how it used to be delivered, and get their views on what they think others would prefer in the future.

- Make other elements of the training relaxed and light-hearted too (for example, using illustrations and animations in any PowerPoint slides, and use colour and illustrations in any pre-course documentation or invitations that are sent out).

Once again I can only reiterate what I said at the beginning of the book, that the use of these methods has, in my experience, made the learning process quicker and more effective than the traditional ways of disseminating knowledge. The activity-based methods are simply just more fun – not only for the learners, but for the trainers too.

If you have found this book useful you may be interested in other titles from Gower

Age Matters:
Employing, Motivating and Managing Older Employees
Keren Smedley and Helen Whitten
978-0-566-08680-9

The CEO:
Chief Engagement Officer
Turning Hierarchy Upside Down to Drive Performance
John Smythe
0 566 08561 5

Handbook of Corporate University Development:
Managing Strategic Learning initiatives in Public and Private Domains
Edited by Rob Paton, Geoff Peters, John Storey and Scott Taylor
978-0-566-08583-3

HR Business Partners
Ian Hunter, Jane Saunders, Allan Boroughs and Simon Constance
978-0-566-08625-0

Management Skills Assessment:
12 Ready-to-Use Audits for Trainers
Mike Woodcock and Dave Francis
978-0-566-08082-1

Practical Succession Management:
How to Future-Proof Your Organization
Andrew Munro
978-0-566-08570-3

GOWER

Requisite Organization:
A Total System for Effective Managerial Organization and
Managerial Leadership for the 21st Century
Elliott Jaques
978-0-566-07940-5

Senior Executive Reward:
Key Models and Practices
Sandy Pepper
978-0-566-08733-2

Strategic HR:
Building the Capability to Deliver
Peter Reilly and Tony Williams
978-0-566-08674-8

Team Metrics:
Resources for Measuring and Improving Team
Performance
Mike Woodcock and Dave Francis
978-0-566-08640-3

Training International Managers:
Designing, Deploying and Delivering Effective Training
for Multi-Cultural Groups
Alan Melkman and John Trotman
978-0-566-08630-4

For further information on these and all our titles visit
our website – www.gowerpub.com
All online orders receive a discount

GOWER

Date Due

IF YOUR BOOK IS RECALLED YOUR DUE
DATE WILL BE SHORTENED. YOU WILL BE
NOTIFIED BY MAIL.